JERRY THOME

LAKE COMO TRAVEL GUIDE 2023, 2024 AND BEYOND

A Traveler's Handbook to Italy's Serene Paradise

Contents

Preface

Walk into the captivating world of Lake Como, a place that draws tourists from all over the world. This scenic refuge, which is tucked away in the Lombardy area of northern Italy, is a true jewel that captures the spirit of unspoiled beauty, vibrant culture, and classic elegance. For centuries, poets, artists, and travelers seeking comfort in its mystical embrace have drawn inspiration from Lake Como, with its shimmering waters, quaint villages, and imposing mansions.

We cordially invite you to set out on an incredible voyage across the marvels of Lake Como with the help of this all-inclusive travel guide. This book will be your reliable travel companion whether you are an experienced tourist or a first-time visitor, pointing out hidden gems and assisting you as you explore the myriad opportunities this breathtaking location has to offer.

We shall reveal Lake Como's mysteries one chapter at a time, beginning with an overview of the area's topography, history, and cultural significance. Take in the captivating stories that have created this region, from the sumptuous Renaissance to the ancient Roman towns, and gain an understanding of the enduring customs that persist to this day.

Our guide will help you plan your trip to Lake Como and make well-informed selections. Find out when is the best time to take in the natural beauty of the area, plan how long to stay, and find out about the different ways you may get to this lakeside haven. Useful information will make your trip easy and hassle-free, such as visa requirements, money conversion, and local customs.

As we explore the cities and villages that line Lake Como's coastline, get ready to be enchanted. From the vibrant city of Como, which acts as the entryway to this magical world, to Bellagio, the "pearl of the lake," each location has a distinct charm that is just waiting to be discovered. Discover architectural wonders, get lost in the small cobblestone streets, and experience the friendly hospitality of the people who live in these villages.

A visit to Lake Como wouldn't be complete without taking in some of its magnificent sites and attractions. Take in the magnificence of Villa del Balbianello, which is situated atop a lush bluff with a view of the lake, or meander through the charming gardens of Villa Carlotta, where art and nature live in perfect harmony. Step inside the sublime Como Cathedral, a stunning specimen of Gothic architecture, and ride the Como-Brunate Funicular for breathtaking panoramic views.

In Lake Como, there are numerous ways to indulge, and delicious food is one of them. Taste the flavors of the area while enjoying mouthwatering cuisine made with ingredients that are acquired locally and freshly. With options ranging from Michelin-starred fine dining to traditional rustic fare, Lake Como's culinary culture is sure to excite your taste buds and leave you craving more.

Our guide will offer you advice on practical ideas and insider recommendations, as well as day outings and excursions to surrounding locations. Wander through the historic alleyways of Bergamo, discover the Swiss beauty of Lugano, or take in the lively energy of Milan. Every trip adds a fresh viewpoint and deepens your comprehension of the surrounding area.

Let your imagination wander to the stunning settings and enthralling activities that await you in Lake Como as you turn the pages of this travel book. Allow the evocative words, breathtaking images, and knowledgeable insights to pique your curiosity and send you on a journey to discover every corner of this enchanted location.

Start your journey today and watch as Lake Como's enchantment materializes before your very eyes.

I

Planning Your Trip

1

A Brief Look into the Past

With its glistening waters and stunning scenery, Lake Como is home to a rich cultural past that extends back thousands of years. This magical location, which is tucked away in the northern Italian province of Lombardy, has captivated travelers from all over the world and shaped the course of history.

There is proof that humans have lived in Lake Como since the Neolithic era, which extends the lake's ancient history. Because of the lake's advantageous location, early civilizations found it to be attractive, and numerous tribes and empires vying for supremacy in the area were drawn to it. Among the first known occupants of Lake Como were the Celts, Romans, and Lombards, all of whom left their cultural imprint.

Lake Como, formerly called "Larius," developed as a major commerce hub during the Roman era. Recognizing the lake's inherent beauty, the Romans built opulent palaces along its banks, some of which survive today as reminders of their magnificence. The peace and breathtaking views that Lake Como provided attracted the Roman nobility, who made the area a popular getaway.

Strong noble families arose in Lake Como during the Middle Ages, competing for dominance and influence over the area. The town of Como's advantageous location along the southwest border of the lake allowed it to grow into a significant hub of industry and trade. The city's vibrant silk industry, which contributed significantly to the region's riches and cultural advancement, was the main driver of its prosperity.

Lake Como underwent an era of spectacular artistic and intellectual development throughout the Renaissance. Leonardo da Vinci, the well-known architect and artist, spent time on the lake's edge, drawing inspiration from its tranquil beauty. As a result of his influence and presence, the area developed into a haven for philosophers, poets, and artists looking for support from affluent noble families and sources of inspiration.

The 18th and 19th centuries saw an increase in the cultural relevance of Lake Como. There was a resurgence of interest in the natural world and the quest for knowledge during the Enlightenment. The ethereal views of the region provided comfort and inspiration to romantic poets and writers like Alessandro Manzoni and Stendhal, who frequently immortalized Lake Como in their writings.

Lake Como saw significant social and industrial transformation during the 19th century. The area became more contemporary during the Industrial Revolution when factories and textile mills sprang up around the lake's edges. The natural beauty of Lake Como and the lavish houses of the rich elite drew a large number of tourists during this industrialization era.

The region became a sought-after resort for the worldwide elite in the 20th century, which only served to heighten Lake Como's attraction. Away from the busy cities and drawn by the picturesque surroundings of the lake, celebrities, politicians, and artists flocked to its shores in search of inspiration. The opulent homes and five-star hotels dotting the area served as playgrounds for the affluent and famous, cementing Lake Como's standing as a representation of elegance and luxury.

Even in modern times, people from all walks of life are still drawn to Lake Como. The region is linked together by its history and cultural heritage, which is evident in its artistic legacy, architectural gems, and friendly locals. Lake Como is a monument to the timeless attractiveness of this magnificent location, from the quaint towns and villages that border its shores to the lavish palaces and verdant gardens that grace its landscapes.

2

The Ideal time to Visit

One of the most important things to think about while making travel plans to Lake Como is when to visit. The region's varied seasons provide one-of-a-kind experiences and charming vistas. The ideal time to visit Lake Como will be discussed in this chapter, with consideration given to the weather, crowd density, and events and activities that are offered at various times of the year.

Spring (March to May): As nature emerges from its winter hibernation, spring is a great time to explore Lake Como. The scenery explodes into a colorful tapestry of trees and flowers in bloom. The average comfortable afternoon temperature rises to between 15°C and 20°C (59°F and 68°F). Even though there are sporadic sprinkles of rain, the weather is usually moderate.

There are fewer visitors to Lake Como in the fall than there are in the summer, so you can take your time exploring the villages and attractions. Enjoy strolls along the lakefront promenades, a visit to the breathtaking Villa Carlotta and Villa Melzi gardens, or a hike along the picturesque hiking trails bordered by thick vegetation. The boating season begins in the spring when you can take leisurely boat rides on the calm lake waters.

Summer (June to August): With good reason, this is Lake Como's busiest travel season. The temperature ranges from 25°C to 30°C (77°F to 86°F) in this pleasant and bright weather. The long days provide lots of chances to enjoy the sun, go boating, and see the area's quaint towns and villages.

The number of visitors increases in tandem with the temperature. Popular vacation spots like Varenna and Bellagio can get very crowded, particularly in July and August. But the energetic atmosphere also makes the area come to life, with a variety of water activities to enjoy, boisterous festivals, and bright outdoor markets. During this busy time, it is important to reserve lodging and activities in advance.

Autumn (September to November): As the scenery turns into a symphony of warm colors, autumn is a wonderful time to take in Lake Como's magnificence. It's the perfect time for outdoor sports and sightseeing because the temperatures are between 15°C and 20°C (59°F and 68°F) and the people start to disperse.

The beautiful autumnal scenery offers an amazing setting for discovery. Enjoy strolls around the lake, trek into the adjacent hills and mountains, or partake in wine sampling at the neighboring vineyards. For those who enjoy the outdoors and taking photos, September and October are especially tempting because of the striking scenery created by the changing leaves.

Winter (December to February): With its serene atmosphere and hint of romance, Lake Como's winter season gives a certain kind of charm. The region receives milder winters than other regions of northern Europe, with temperatures ranging from 0°C to 10°C (32°F to 50°F).

At this time of year, Lake Como has a more sedate vibe because fewer people are visiting the area. With their holiday decorations, mulled wine aromas, and Christmas markets, the towns and villages radiate a warm and inviting charm. Enjoy the peace and quiet of the lake's winter splendor, stroll quietly down the shore, and tour the historic attractions without the crowds.

It's crucial to remember that some hotels and attractions can have restricted winter hours or closures, so it's best to check before and make plans appropriately.

3

Navigating Lake Como

When organizing your journey to this alluring location, transportation to and around Lake Como is a crucial component. Located in the northern Italian province of Lombardy, Lake Como has a variety of transportation choices to facilitate travel throughout the area and is well-connected to major cities. This chapter will cover how to get to Lake Como as well as the several ways to get around the lake and see its charming villages and stunning scenery.

Below are the following ways to travel to Lake Como:

1. **By Air**: Flying into one of the local airports is the most practical way to get to Lake Como from overseas locations. Milan Malpensa Airport, which is roughly 45 kilometers (28 miles) from Como, is the closest. It is a significant global hub with connections to many cities across the globe. Milan Linate Airport, which is located roughly 70 kilometers (43 miles) from Como, is an additional choice. Buses, trains, and taxis are among the modes of transportation available from both airports to get to Lake Como.

2. **By Train:** Train travel is a practical choice because Lake Como is well-connected to the Italian rail system. The primary train station in the city of Como, Como San Giovanni, is a significant center for transit. Como is easily accessible by train, which operates frequently from Milan and other important Italian towns. From Como San Giovanni, it's simple to travel by bus, train, or boat to other towns surrounding the lake.

3. **By Car**: Getting to Lake Como by car is a feasible choice for tourists who value their freedom. The A9 freeway, which links Como to Milan and other important Italian cities, provides access to the area. It should be noted that driving in towns like Como's historic areas might be difficult because of the small streets and little parking. Nonetheless, there are plenty of parking lots outside of the city centers, from which you may use public transportation to further explore the region.

The available modes of transportation to navigate Lake Como are as follows:

1. **By Bus:** There is an extensive bus network around Lake Como that makes traveling throughout the area easy. The smaller villages and larger towns are connected by buses, which provide an affordable mode of transportation. Access to expansive views and undiscovered treasures can be had via the bus routes that travel across the neighboring hills and lakefront locations. Combining several forms of transportation is made simple by the bus services' dependability and coordination with boat schedules.

2. **By Train**: Another option to go around Lake Como is via the

train system. The municipalities of Lecco, Bellano, and Colico are connected to Como by train services run by the Ferrovie Nord Milano (FN). For tourists who are staying in Como and touring the eastern beaches of the lake, trains provide a rapid and economical means of transportation between locations. There are regular train schedules, and tickets are available online or at the stations.

3. **By Boat:** Traveling around Lake Como by boat is among the most picturesque and entertaining options. A vast network of ferries links the major towns and villages situated along the lake's shore. Ferries provide a relaxing and scenic ride that lets you take in the breathtaking scenery and the opulent mansions that line the coast. You may catch a ferry from Como to places like Bellagio, Varenna, and Menaggio. Seasonal variations in ferry service frequency include more departures in the summer.

4. **On Foot**: It's best to explore Lake Como's towns and villages on foot to take in the picturesque streets, important historical buildings, and breathtaking vistas at your own pace. The lakefront promenades provide enjoyable strolling paths that link different attractions and allow unhindered views of the lake. Hiking enthusiasts can enjoy exploring beautiful routes with expansive views of the lake and the Alps as they travel through the nearby hills.

5. **Rental Cars and Taxis**: Although public transit is widely accessible and practical, some travelers might value the independence of having their vehicle. Airports and large cities rent automobiles, giving you the flexibility to see Lake Como and its surroundings at your speed. It's crucial to remember that

navigating Lake Como's twisting, tiny roads can be difficult, particularly during the hot summer months when traffic jams are frequent.

Additionally, taxis are widely accessible throughout the area, offering a practical choice for quick excursions or transportation to particular locations. Taxis are available at town centers, airports, and train stations. It is advisable to ask the driver to confirm the fare before setting off on your trip.

4

Entry Requirements

To guarantee a hassle-free and seamless admission into Italy and Lake Como, it is imperative to comprehend the entry criteria before starting your visit. Here, we'll go over the various nationalities' visa requirements and offer broad advice on how to get a visa to visit Lake Como.

Italy, which includes Lake Como, is a member of the Schengen Area, a group of 26 European nations where internal borders have been eliminated. Visa-free travel into the Schengen Area is granted to nationals of numerous nations, including the US, Canada, Australia, and the majority of EU member states, for tourism and leisure activities. Generally, visitors from these nations are permitted up to 90 days of stay within 180 days in the Schengen Area, which includes Italy.

The following are typical instances of nations whose nationals are permitted entry into Lake Como for up to 90 days during 180 days without a visa:

- Canada and the United States
- Australia
- Korea, S.
- Chile
- United Kingdom
- Argentina

This is not a complete list, therefore it's crucial to confirm the most recent requirements for your nationality's type of visa.

Nationals of nations exempt from visa requirements can travel to Lake Como without requiring a visa. When they get to the Italian border, their passports are stamped with the entrance date, granting them entry. It's crucial to remember that you still need a valid passport and that it must be valid for at least six months after the date you plan to depart.

To visit Lake Como, if you are a citizen of a nation that is not on the list of nations exempt from requiring a visa, you must apply for a Schengen visa. You can travel for work or pleasure within the Schengen Area with a Schengen visa. You must apply for a Schengen visa at the Italian consulate or embassy of your nation of origin or the nation in which you now reside legally.

Typically, obtaining a Schengen visa requires submitting the following paperwork:

- Filled out application for a visa.
- A valid passport that has at least two blank pages and is valid for an additional six months after the date of scheduled

departure.
- Current passport-sized photos.
- Evidence of travel plans, such as airline tickets and itineraries.
- Proof of lodging, such as hotel bookings or a letter of invitation from a host in Italy.
- Medical costs and repatriation are covered by travel medical insurance, with a minimum coverage of €30,000 (or equivalent).
- Provide evidence of adequate finances to support your stay in Italy, such as a sponsorship letter or bank statements.
- Evidence of your plan to return home following your visit, such as a letter of employment, property ownership, or family ties.

It's crucial to remember that the consulate or embassy where you apply may have slightly different procedures for applying for a visa. It is important to visit the official website of the Italian embassy or consulate in your nation to verify the precise requirements and procedures.

You must apply for the proper visa or residence permit in advance if you intend to stay in Lake Como or Italy for a longer period than is allowed without a visa, such as for employment, study, or long-term residency. Depending on why you are visiting, these visas and permits have different requirements and application processes. It is advisable to seek advice and thorough information on the particular visa or permission you need from the Italian embassy or consulate that is closest to you.

5

Financial Matters

When making travel plans to Lake Como, it's critical to be aware of the local currency, banking options, and helpful money management advice. To ensure that your visit goes smoothly and conveniently, this chapter will present you with important information about currency matters.

Italy, which includes Lake Como, uses the Euro (€) as its official currency. Transactions and purchases are made simply by the widespread acceptance of the Euro throughout the region. When dealing with tiny sellers, local markets, or institutions that might not accept credit or debit cards, it is helpful to have the local money on hand. To ensure you have currency on hand, try to get some euros either before you leave or when you get to the airport.

Exchange offices, banks, airports, and certain hotels in the larger cities surrounding Lake Como offer currency exchange services. To make sure you get the best value for your money, it is advised to compare exchange rates and costs. While they might impose a modest commission, banks normally provide competitive rates. The convenience of extended hours and multiple locations is offered by exchange offices, notwithstanding their potentially higher prices.

ATMs are widely distributed in Lake Como and are known as "Bancomats" in Italy. They give you an easy option to take out cash straight from your bank account in the local currency. Banks, retail establishments, and town centers all have ATMs. For security reasons, it's crucial to let your bank or credit card company know when you'll be traveling so they don't block your cards. Remember that there can be a price associated with using an ATM. It is best to inquire with your bank about any fees that apply and to take out bigger amounts to save transaction costs.

Visa and Mastercard are generally accepted in Lake Como, particularly at larger venues such as restaurants and hotels. Primary credit cards like Visa and Mastercard are widely accepted, but in case of any technical difficulties, it's wise to always have a backup card from an alternate supplier. It's advisable to have your passport, or a photocopy of it, on you in case you're questioned for identification when using your card. To prevent any potential card blocking due to suspected fraudulent activity, let your card issuer know about your trip intentions.

Please also bear in mind that you should give safety and security a priority when managing your money and financial affairs. Just bring the cash you'll need for everyday expenses, and keep it safe in a hidden pocket or money belt. Avoid flashing valuables or big sums of cash in public and be aware of your surroundings.

Use ATMs in well-lit, high-traffic areas whenever possible, and stay alert to avoid being robbed or duped.

Italy does not tip as much as some other countries, and this includes Lake Como. It is valued for the outstanding service, nonetheless. Rounding up the check or leaving a little tip as a sign of gratitude is standard practice in restaurants. It's wise to double-check the bill before adding a gratuity because it can already include a service charge. Leaving a little change as a tip is customary at cafes and bars. Although rounding up the fare is customary, tipping taxi drivers is not required.

6

Safety Measures

E ven though Lake Como is a typically safe area to visit, it's still crucial to put your safety first and take the appropriate safety steps to guarantee a hassle-free and joyful experience. These safety recommendations will enable you to enjoy water sports, hike in the mountains, or explore lakefront towns to the fullest while being safe.

1. **Be Aware of Water Safety**: Due to the size of Lake Como, care must be taken when participating in water activities. If you're not a confident swimmer, you might want to use other flotation devices or wear a life jacket. Observe any signage or cautions about deep waters, currents, or spots that are off-limits to swimming. Additionally, it's a good idea to swim in approved regions and stay away from swimming alone, particularly in far or unmonitored areas.

2. **Stay Aware of Your Environment**: Although Lake Como is a typically safe place to visit, it's crucial to be mindful of your surroundings, especially in busy tourist areas. Always keep a

watch on your possessions, and exercise vigilance in populated areas where pickpocketing may occur, such as bustling streets, train stations, or marketplaces. Respect your personal space and refrain from interacting with shady people or taking advantage of uninvited offers.

3. **Hike responsibly**: There are several beautiful hiking trails around Lake Como. Be sure that you are well-prepared before embarking on a hike. Carry a map or guidebook, bring enough water, and wear appropriate footwear. Follow approved paths; do not go into uncharted or isolated places by yourself. Consider checking the weather forecast and packing for any changes in circumstances if you intend to hike in the mountains. Tell someone when you plan to hike and when you expect to return.

4. **Stay Safe on the Road:** Get acquainted with the traffic laws and ordinances in the area if you intend to drive via Lake Como. When driving on twisting roads, especially in mountainous locations, pay attention to speed limits and drive carefully. Certain towns may have restricted parking, so it's best to park in approved spots and keep your distance from narrow streets. If you're not comfortable driving, you may move around the area via buses, trains, and boats as well as other public transit.

5. **Drink plenty of water and shield yourself from the sun**: Lake Como can get very hot in the summer. Drinking lots of water throughout the day is crucial to staying hydrated, especially if you're participating in outdoor activities. Sunglasses, a hat, and sunscreen are good ways to shield your skin from UV radiation. To prevent overheating, seek shade during the warmest parts of the day and take rests in cool, well-ventilated settings.

6. **Honor Local Traditions and Culture:** Because Lake Como is a culturally and historically diverse area, it's critical to honor its customs and traditions. Learn the fundamentals of Italian politeness, such as saying "Buongiorno" (good morning) or "Buona sera" (good evening) to strangers. Don't wear anything too exposing and dress modestly when you attend churches or other places of worship. Additionally, it is courteous to obtain consent before snapping pictures, especially in places of worship or privacy.

7. **Keep Up with the Weather**: Lake Como has a range of temperatures all year long. To make sure you are ready for the weather, check the local weather prediction before your trip. Plan your activities following any probable weather alerts or warnings, such as those regarding thunderstorms or excessive rainfall. When participating in outdoor activities like hiking or boating, pay attention to the weather and take the necessary safety precautions.

8. **Emergency Contacts and Travel Insurance are King:** Before your journey, write down the phone numbers of local law enforcement, hospitals, and your embassy or consulate in case of an emergency. For example, in Lake Como, the common emergency ambulance service number is 118. Having travel insurance that covers medical costs, trip cancellations, and lost or stolen luggage is also advised. Learn the ins and outs of your insurance policy so you can be sure you have enough protection while traveling.

9. **Use Caution with Food and Water**: Although Lake Como often upholds strict guidelines for the safety of food and water,

it's still essential to use caution, particularly when eating at neighborhood restaurants or drinking tap water. Remain with respectable eateries and restaurants that follow appropriate sanitary standards. Use bottled water or water purification techniques, such as boiling or utilizing pills, if you're not confident about the quality of the water.

7

Useful Phrases in Italian

It's always a good idea to brush up on some basic Italian words before you travel to the stunning Lake Como in Italy. Even if English is often spoken by residents in tourist destinations, trying to speak Italian will not only improve your experience but also demonstrate respect for the local way of life. Here are a few keywords and phrases to assist you in finding this fascinating place.

Greetings and Basic Phrases
1. Buongiorno! - Good morning!
2. Buonasera! - Good evening!
3. Ciao! - Hello/Hi (informal)
4. Grazie - Thank you
5. Prego - You're welcome
6. Mi scusi - Excuse me
7. Per favore - Please
8. Scusa/Scusami - Sorry/Excuse me (informal)
9. Non capisco - I don't understand
10. Parla inglese? - Do you speak English?

Phrases to help you gain direction

11. Dov'è...? - Where is...?

12. A sinistra - To the left

13. A Destra - To the right

14. Posso avere indicazioni per...? - Can I have directions to...?

15. Quanto costa? - How much does it cost?

16. Vorrei prenotare un taxi - I would like to book a taxi

17..Avanti - Straight ahead

18. Quanto dista...? - How far is...?

If you're eating out

19. Un tavolo per due, per favore - A table for two, please

20..Il menu, per favore - The menu, please

21. Cosa mi consiglia? - What do you recommend?

22. Vorrei ordinare... - I would like to order...

23. Il conto, per favore - The bill, please

24. Posso pagare con carta di credito? - Can I pay with a credit card?

Shopping

25. Quanto costa? - How much does it cost?

26. Acqua naturale/gassata - Still/sparkling water

27. Mi piace molto! - I like it!

28. Posso provare questo? - Can I try this on?

29. Avete qualcosa di meno costoso? - Do you have something cheaper?

30. Posso pagare con carta di debito? - Can I pay with a debit card?

For when you're in an emergency:

31. Aiuto! - Help!

32. Ho perso il mio passaporto - I lost my passport
33. Dov'è la Stazione di polizia? - Where is the police station?
34. Chiamate un'ambulanza! - Call an ambulance!
35. Ho bisogno di un dottore - I need a doctor

Miscellaneous:

36. Vorrei prenotare un hotel - I would like to book a hotel
37. Qual è il tuo nome? - What is your name? (informal)
38. Buon viaggio! - Have a good trip!
39. Dov'è il bagno? - Where is the bathroom?
40. Mi potete consigliare un buon ristorante? - Can you recommend a good restaurant?

Gaining some basic Italian language skills will help you have a more pleasurable trip to Lake Como. You'll feel more a part of the community and the culture, and the locals will appreciate your effort. Don't forget to fully absorb the allure of this magnificent location while assiduously learning the native tongue.

Buon viaggio! (Have a good trip!)

II

Lake Como's Notable Towns

8

Como

C omo is a charming town situated at the southern extremity of Lake Como. It's recognized for its gorgeous location, historic charm, and active vibe. The town emanates a sense of grandeur with its scenic shoreline, medieval buildings, and majestic mountain backdrop. At the heart of Como sits its namesake, Lake Como, which contributes to the town's charm.

One of the town's highlights is the Cathedral of Como, an architectural marvel exhibiting a blend of Gothic and Renaissance styles. Its elaborate façade and magnificent interior with ornate artwork and sculptures draw people from all over the world. Adjacent to the cathedral is the Broletto, a medieval town hall that adds to Como's historical richness.

Exploring the town on foot is a lovely experience. Piazza Cavour serves as a focal hub bursting with activity, lined with cafes and restaurants where visitors can sample local food while observing the dynamic environment. The town's picturesque streets provide a mix of boutique shops, craft stores, and local markets, great for strolls and purchasing unusual souvenirs.

For a panoramic perspective of Como and its surrounding splendor, a visit to Brunat is a must. Accessible by funicular, Brunate offers stunning panoramas of the lake and the town below, giving it a perfect site for photographers and wildlife enthusiasts.

Como's history with silk manufacture is visible in its Silk Museum (Museo della Seta), exhibiting the town's historical role in the silk industry. Visitors can dig into the intricate process of silk production and its impact on Como's economy and culture.

Boat cruises are a popular way to enjoy the beauty of Lake Como, and Como serves as a good starting place. Visitors can embark on leisurely cruises, enjoying the lake's breathtaking magnificence, and visiting other attractive cities like Bellagio, Varenna, or Tremezzo.

Lastly, Como holds a range of events throughout the year, from cultural festivals to art exhibitions and musical concerts. The Como Film Festival and Settimane Musicali di Como (Como Musical Weeks) are among the prominent events that attract art and culture fans.

Overall, Como's blend of history, natural beauty, and cultural diversity makes it a mesmerizing destination that leaves a lasting impact on every visitor.

9

Varenna

Varenna, a charming village set along the eastern side of Lake Como, is a gorgeous treasure recognized for its calm beauty, historical significance, and romantic ambiance. Its picturesque streets, colorful buildings, and breathtaking lakeside vistas make it a quintessential destination for those seeking an authentic Italian experience.

Varenna's charm rests in its pristine beauty and quiet ambiance. The village is characterized by tiny cobblestone lanes that weave their way up from the lakeshore, adorned with bright flowers falling from balconies. The stunning vistas of the crystal-clear waters of Lake Como against the backdrop of the lush foliage and towering mountains create a calm mood that captivates visitors.

One of Varenna's main attractions is the Villa Monastero. This exquisite mansion, previously a Cistercian cloister, shows a stunning blend of art, history, and botanical wonders.

The villa's stunning grounds, boasting a diverse array of plant species, attract guests with their beauty and peacefulness. The picturesque promenade along the lake allows tourists to explore this architectural jewel while appreciating the stunning views.

Overlooking Varenna lies the Castello di Vezio, a historic fortress built by the Lombard Queen Theodelinda, giving magnificent panoramas of Lake Como.

'Ghost' of Castello di Vezio

Visitors can embark on a picturesque climb up to the castle, exploring its historic walls, towers, and dungeons. The panoramic views from the castle's vantage point are just amazing, giving a great environment for capturing stunning images and immersing oneself in the natural splendor of the environs.

The Church of San Giorgio is a historic site in Varenna, showing a blend of Romanesque and Gothic architectural styles. Its simplicity and elegance add to the village's attractiveness. Nearby, Piazza San Giorgio offers a great area to relax and soak in the local ambiance.

Visitors can have a relaxing coffee or a meal at one of the cafes while observing the gorgeous surroundings.

From Varenna, travelers have easy access to different excursions on Lake Como. Ferry cruises enable for exploration of surrounding cities like Bellagio and Menaggio, allowing an opportunity to view the lake's grandeur from new perspectives. Water sports aficionados can engage in activities such as kayaking, paddleboarding, or simply having a refreshing swim in the clean waters of the lake.

Throughout the year, Varenna holds many cultural events and festivities that bring liveliness to the town. The Varenna-Esino Lario Festival presents a blend of music, art, and local traditions, attracting both locals and tourists alike. Additionally, the hamlet celebrates religious and historical occasions with fervor, allowing tourists a chance to immerse themselves in the local culture and traditions.

Varenna's breathtaking beauty and serene environment make it a perfect destination for those seeking a peaceful vacation amidst nature's majesty. The village's rich history, gorgeous vistas, and genuine welcome offer an unforgettable experience for those who visit its picturesque coastlines.

10

Menaggio

The quaint village of Menaggio, which is located on the western edge of Lake Como, has the ideal fusion of energetic energy, historical charm, and scenic beauty. Thanks to its gorgeous lakefront, easy access to other well-known locations, and charming waterfront, Menaggio has grown to be a well-liked destination for travelers looking for a fun getaway near Lake Como.

The vista of vibrant houses surrounding Lake Como's beaches, with the towering mountains providing a striking backdrop, welcomes you as you reach Menaggio. The town's convenient lakeside position makes it a great starting point for exploring the area, and its hospitable environment puts you at ease the moment you arrive.

Piazza Garibaldi, a picturesque plaza and the lively center of Menaggio, is the town's heart. A lovely mix of cafes, gelaterias, boutiques, and restaurants can be found here.

Grab a seat on one of the outside patios and indulge in a delectable gelato or cappuccino while taking in the vibrant atmosphere. The 16th-century Church of Santo Stefano, a stunning example of Renaissance architecture that is well worth a visit, is located on the square as well.

Menaggio's charming lakefront promenade, which spans along the waterfront and provides expansive views of the lake and the surrounding mountains, is one of the town's highlights. Enjoy the peace of the lake and the fresh air by taking a stroll down the promenade. There are benches all along the promenade, which make it ideal to sit and enjoy the beautiful scenery or just watch the boats sail across the glistening seas.

A trip to the Castello di Menaggio is essential for history buffs. Located atop a hill with a stunning view of the town, this ancient fortification provides insight into the area's fascinating history. Discover its historic walls, ascend the tower for sweeping views, and become engrossed in Menaggio's past. In addition, the castle holds exhibitions and cultural events that deepen one's awareness of the town's past.

There is a lot for outdoor enthusiasts to discover in and around Menaggio. Hiking, biking, and outdoor experiences abound on the town's picturesque paths, rolling hills, and verdant surroundings. The scenic Greenway del Lago di Como, which links Menaggio with other towns like Cadenabbia and Griante, is one well-liked pathway. Wander along the trail and enjoy breathtaking views of tranquil lakes, quaint villages, and peaceful scenery.

You can reach the renowned Villa Carlotta in Tremezzo with a quick boat journey from Menaggio. This magnificent home is well known for its breathtaking grounds, which are home to numerous exotic plants, vivid flowers, and imposing statues. Enjoy the splendor of the well-planned gardens and the serene atmosphere that permeates the estate as you take a stroll around the grounds.

Take a boat journey to the neighboring cities and villages to appreciate Lake Como's charm. It's simple to go from Menaggio to well-known locations like Bellagio, Varenna, and Como. Take a ferry ride and enjoy the stunning views of the lake while cruising across the immaculate waters. Stop at several ports to discover the distinct beauty of each location.

Menaggio provides a variety of gastronomic treats for dining. There is plenty to suit every appetite, from classic trattorias offering hearty Italian cuisine to sophisticated lakefront restaurants serving gourmet cuisine. Savor locally produced cheeses, freshly caught seafood, and risotto while sipping on a glass of excellent Italian wine. Menaggio's food scene bears witness to the region's rich culinary history.

Menaggio holds several festivals and events all year long to highlight its rich traditions and culture. Every summer, the world-famous artists who perform at the Menaggio Guitar Festival enthrall music lovers with their enthralling performances.

A bustling environment is created by live music and food vendors along the streets during the Menaggio Street Food Festival, which offers a gourmet trip via both local and foreign flavors. These gatherings give you a chance to interact with the lively Menaggio community and become fully immersed in the local way of life.

A mystical glow descends upon Menaggio as the sun sets. A pleasant glow covers the town as the gentle golden light bounces off the sea. This is the ideal moment to unwind at a lakefront cafe, enjoy a glass of wine, and take in the serene beauty of Lake Como while the hues of the sky merge.

Menaggio's captivating beauty and friendly warmth will stay with you long after it's time to say goodbye. The town's picturesque location, fascinating history, and lively atmosphere combine to make for an amazing experience that will stay with you long after you've left.

Menaggio provides the ideal combination of leisure and discovery thanks to its breathtaking vistas, alluring historical district, and easy access to other important locations. You can enjoy the taste of real Italian food, learn about the history of the area, and become fully immersed in the natural beauty of Lake Como.

11

Lecco

T ravelers looking for a distinctive Italian experience should not miss the town of Lecco, which is perched at the southernmost point of the stunning Lake Como. Lecco provides visitors with an enthralling fusion of old-world charm and contemporary attraction thanks to its breathtaking natural surroundings, extensive history, and lively environment.

Situated 50 kilometers northeast of Milan, Lecco is a picturesque town encircled by towering mountains and glistening lakes. The hamlet provides visitors with an alternative viewpoint of the area's splendor by acting as a gateway to Lake Como's eastern branch. Beautiful views of the glistening lake, dense vegetation, and tall peaks will welcome you as you get closer to Lecco and create the mood for an amazing journey.

Lecco's scenic Lungolago waterfront promenade, which runs along the lake's eastern bank, is one of the city's most notable attractions. Strolling down this quaint path will let you take in the tranquil atmosphere and see expansive views of the surrounding lake and mountains in the distance. Vibrant cafes, restaurants, and boutiques line the Lungolago, making it the ideal place to indulge in regional fare or go souvenir shopping.

You will come across many beautiful architectural structures as you stroll around Lecco's old town. The town's remarkable collection of Art Nouveau and Neoclassical structures offers a window into its illustrious past. See the stunning Palazzo delle Paure, a stately mansion that is home to the Historical Archive and Civic Art Gallery. Enter to view a stunning collection of artwork that includes pieces by Italian masters and regional artists.

A trip to the Museo Manzoniano is essential for those interested in learning more about Lecco's past. Honoring the great Italian writer Alessandro Manzoni, who brought fame and glory to the town with his well-known book "The Betrothed," this museum provides insightful information on the life and works of the renowned writer. Explore Lecco's literary past by meandering through halls brimming with first drafts, individual items, and moving displays.

Around Lecco, outdoor enthusiasts will have no shortage of activities to enjoy. Due to the town's advantageous location at the base of the Alps, there are many hiking and climbing options nearby. Enter the magnificent Resegone Regional Park and follow the picturesque trails that lead to alpine meadows and panoramic vistas. As an alternative, explore the quaint villages along the lake's edge by boat.

The magnificent waters of Lake Como draw travelers, and Lecco provides ample opportunity to enjoy them. Take a boat tour to see the magnificent houses and gardens that border the lake, or rent a kayak or paddleboard to explore it on your own. A dash of rustic beauty is added by the surrounding village of Pescarenico, with its small alleys and colorful fishermen's dwellings.

Lecco also organizes a range of annual cultural events. Music festivals, art shows, and customary festivities that highlight the region's colorful past are all part of the bustling city calendar. Early December brings the San Nicolò Festival, which is not to be missed. Food vendors, live music, and an amazing fireworks display fill the streets.

Lecco has a delicious selection of food options when it comes to dining. Savor regional specialties like polenta uncia, a typical dish made with cornmeal and cheese, or missoltini, dried and grilled lake fish. For a genuinely realistic dining experience, pair your meal with a glass of Valtellina wine, which is produced in the neighboring Lombardy area.

12

Tremezzo

Situated on the western bank of Lake Como, the charming village of Tremezzo presents an alluring fusion of luxurious houses, exquisite gardens, and breathtaking views of the lake. Travelers looking for a taste of luxury and scenic beauty are drawn to Tremezzo because of its alluring ambiance and rich cultural legacy.

Upon arriving at Tremezzo, you will be welcomed by the sight of opulent hotels and villas scattered around the coastline. The village, with its colorful flowers, immaculate gardens, and a backdrop of rolling hills and breathtaking mountains, emanates sophistication and elegance. Tremezzo is a great place for people looking for historical and natural wonders because it is home to some of Lake Como's most recognizable landmarks.

It is essential to visit the neighboring hillside village of Tremezzina if you are looking for panoramic views. You will be rewarded with breathtaking views of Lake Como, the surrounding Alps, and the nearby villages as you ascend the twisting roads. Seize the opportunity to appreciate the breathtaking scenery and record the picture-perfect vistas that Tremezzo has to offer.

Tremezzo's lakefront promenade is a lovely spot to decompress and take in the laid-back vibe. Enjoy the calm wind and the soothing sound of the water lapping against the shore as you stroll idly around the lake. Admire the well-designed houses that border the shore; some have been turned into opulent hotels that offer a taste of life at a higher level. Enjoy a delectable meal or a cool drink at one of the little cafés or eateries along the promenade while taking in the alluring scenery.

There is a lot for outdoor enthusiasts to discover in and around Tremezzo. The community provides hiking, mountain biking, and rock climbing activities as well as access to the breathtaking peaks of the Grigne Mountains. Take a stroll and you'll be rewarded with expansive views of the lake and the verdant surroundings.

Tremezzo is the starting point for a short boat ride to the quaint village of Bellagio, sometimes referred to as the "Pearl of Lake Como." With the lake and mountains as a backdrop, this charming location features charming boutiques, old houses, and winding cobblestone alleyways. Discover secret spots, take your time exploring the hamlet, and enjoy the genuine Italian charm that permeates Bellagio's streets.

Tremezzo has several different gastronomic treats to choose from when it comes to dining. There is a restaurant or trattoria to suit every taste, ranging from classy lakeside eateries to intimate ones. Savor local delicacies including freshly caught lake fish, freshly cooked pasta, and rich pastries. Enjoy a glass of the region's wine with your dinner and let the tastes of Tremezzo entice your senses.

Tremezzo holds a number of festivals and events all year long to highlight its rich traditions and culture. Talented artists from all over the world come together for the Tremezzo Music Festival, which enthralls audiences with classical and modern performances in breathtaking settings. Every year, the Tremezzo Wine Festival honors the area's history of winemaking and provides a chance to taste a range of regional wines and discover the craft of viticulture.

The allure of Tremezzo goes beyond its breathtaking scenery and varied cultural offers. The community also offers a variety of lodging choices, ranging from opulent hotels on the lake to charming bed & breakfasts. Take in a leisurely breakfast while taking in the expansive vistas as you awaken to the tranquil murmur of the lake. The lodging options at Tremezzo offer the ideal balance of style and comfort, guaranteeing a delightful stay along Lake Como's shores.

13

Cernobbio

The majestic Villa d'Este is one of Cernobbio's most recognizable sights.

This opulent palace, which dates to the 16th century, was formerly the home of nobility and is currently a five-star hotel. Villa d'Este, which is surrounded by immaculate grounds, has stunning architecture, elaborate interiors, and awe-inspiring lake vistas. Take in the fragrance of blossoming flowers as you stroll through its magnificent gardens and picture the grandeur of a bygone period.

The Cernobbio lakefront promenade provides a serene environment for admiring Lake Como's splendor. Admire the exquisite villas that line the waterfront as you stroll idly along the waterfront. The promenade is lined with quaint cafes, gelaterias, and restaurants where you can take a break to savor a delectable meal or a cup of coffee while taking in the tranquil lake views. Settle down on a bench and enjoy the soothing touch of a light breeze while admiring the captivating views of the surrounding mountains and passing boats.

Numerous attractions are available in Cernobbio for those looking for cultural experiences. See the Chiesa di San Vincenzo, a church from the fourteenth century with exquisite murals and architectural details. Another famous villa in Cernobbio is the Villa Bernasconi, which holds cultural events and art exhibitions that shed light on the artistic legacy of the area. In addition, the village has a variety of stores and boutiques where you can peruse items made locally, including clothing, souvenirs, and crafts.

There are lots of opportunities for nature lovers to explore Cernobbio's surrounding landscapes. The Monte Bisbino mountain, which has hiking trails with expansive views of the lake and the surrounding valleys, is not far from the village.

Take a stroll through the verdant forests, take in the clean mountain air, and savor the peace of the natural world. Additionally, the Monte Bisbino offers a wonderful vantage point for taking in Lake Como's beauty from above.

Cernobbio is the starting point for a short drive to the lake's largest city, Como. Discover the quaint squares, winding streets, and medieval architecture of Como's historic center.

Throughout the year, Cernobbio hosts several events and festivals that add a touch of vibrancy to the village. The Cernobbio Music Festival brings together talented musicians from around the world, enchanting audiences with captivating performances in unique venues. The Cernobbio Flower Festival showcases exquisite floral displays, transforming the village into a riot of colors and scents. These events provide a wonderful opportunity to immerse yourself in the local culture, celebrate the beauty of nature, and connect with the warm-hearted community of Cernobbio.

III

Top Attractions and Destinations

A lot of these places and attractions have been mentioned in the previous section. In this new section, we'll be giving you a bit more information about them. Enjoy!

14

Villa del Balbianello

Villa del Balbianello is a stunning example of the fusion of great architecture and breathtaking surroundings. It is situated atop a picturesque bluff with a view of Lake Como's dazzling waves. Situated in the village of Lenno on the western shore of Lake Como, this exquisite home is a must-visit for anyone seeking to immerse themselves in the timeless charm of the lake.

Constructed in the 18th century as a Franciscan monastery, Villa del Balbianello underwent numerous alterations throughout the years until it was acquired by Italian adventurer Guido Monzino in 1974. Driven by his love of art and collecting, Monzino meticulously restored the villa, transforming it into a private residence showcasing his extensive collection of artwork, antiques, and artifacts.

Approaching Villa del Balbianello is an experience unlike any other. Situated solely on the lake by boat, visitors can expect an idyllic journey over the blue waters of Lake Como, surrounded by lush mountains and charming villages by the shore. As soon as you walk off the boat at the villa's private pier, you're surrounded by an aura of elegance and peace.

The villa's architectural design blends in perfectly with the surroundings, creating a visually appealing blend of man-made and natural components. The tiered gardens are expertly constructed and meander down the slope, offering breathtaking views at every turn. They are filled with vibrant flowers, old trees, and well-kept hedges. Take a stroll through the gardens, making stops to see the beautiful fountains, statues, and charming stone pathways that lead to hidden alcoves and lakefront overlooks.

One of Villa del Balbianello's most distinctive features is the regal loggia. This outdoor gallery offers expansive vistas of Lake Como and the neighboring Alps, thanks to its sweeping colonnades. It's been the background for many films, such as "Casino Royale" and "Star Wars: Episode II - Attack of the Clones." Standing on the loggia, you are captivated by the alluring beauty surrounding you.

As soon as you walk into the villa, you are thrust into an extravagant and historically significant world. Every interior area is a veritable treasure mine of art, each with its unique charm. Admire the exquisite woodwork, tapestries, and stunning ceilings as you go through the hallways. Monzino's collection of artifacts provides an insight into the rich history of exploration and discovery, encompassing everything from historical papers to navigational tools.

Villa del Balbianello is renowned not just for its exquisite artwork and architectural marvels but also for its seductive ambiance. Over the years, a number of well-known people have been drawn to this picturesque location, including writers, artists, and even kings. To further enhance its romantic appeal, the villa's captivating charm has made it a favorite option for weddings and other special occasions.

A trip to Villa del Balbianello offers pop culture aficionados and movie buffs an opportunity to explore the world of movies. Discover the sites of famous scenes, such as the romantic balcony where Padmé Amidala and Anakin Skywalker spent a passionate moment in "Star Wars." Take in the enchantment of these motion picture moments and make your memories in these sacred spaces.

As your time at Villa del Balbianello draws to an end, pause to appreciate the beauty and peace of the area. Take in the fresh air, relax on a bench with a view of the lake, and feel the calm atmosphere wash over you. Consider the centuries of history that Villa del Balbianello has seen, as well as its eternal elegance. This exceptional site offers a unique experience, regardless of your interests—art, nature, or just some quiet time.

Make sure to stop by the gift shop at Villa del Balbianello before you leave, as it offers a variety of handcrafted crafts, literature, and unique gifts that are inspired by the villa and its environs. Bring a bit of its splendor with you so that the memories will last long after you've departed.

15

Villa Carlotta

V illa Carlotta, which is situated on the western edge of Lake Como, is a magnificent example of art, architecture, and the harmony of nature. Travelers looking to experience the allure of Lake Como should make time to view this exquisite property, which is situated in the quaint village of Tremezzo.

Villa Carlotta was named for Carlotta, the daughter of Princess

Marianne of Nassau and the bride of George II, Duke of Sachsen-Meiningen, and was constructed at the end of the 17th century by a Milanese marquis. The villa was owned by various families before the Clerici family bought it and brought their passion for art and the outdoors into it. Currently open to the public as a museum and botanical garden, Villa Carlotta captivates guests with its sumptuous interiors and breathtaking exteriors.

The magnificent front of Villa Carlotta greets you as you approach; it is a masterwork of architecture that skillfully combines romantic and neoclassical elements. The estate is encircled by exquisitely tended grounds that are full of colorful flowers, old trees, and aromatic citrus orchards. Entering will take you to a realm of exquisite style and creative magnificence.

Villa Carlotta's interior is a veritable gold mine of artwork and antiques. Rich collections of sculptures, paintings, and furniture from different eras are on display in each area. Explore the corridors of this magnificent home and take in the delicate stucco work, gorgeous ceilings, and exquisite tapestries. A great highlight is the Sala degli Specchi, or Hall of Mirrors, with its brilliant mirrors reflecting the light of the day and evoking a magical mood.

The art gallery, which holds an impressive collection of sculptures by well-known artists including Antonio Canova and Bertel Thorvaldsen, is one of Villa Carlotta's most important attractions. Admire Canova's famous sculpture "Amore e Psiche" (Cupid and Psyche), which perfectly embodies the mythological figures' timeless beauty and nuanced feelings. The exhibition also features beautiful paintings that highlight the region's rich artistic legacy, such as those by Francesco Hayez and Jean-Baptiste Wicar.

For those who enjoy the outdoors, Villa Carlotta's botanical gardens are an absolute pleasure. The gardens, which cover an area of more than 70,000 square meters, are a stunning example of botanical diversity, with a vast array of different plants, flowers, and trees from all over the world. Enjoy a stroll through the gardens and let yourself be enchanted by the aromatic flowers, peaceful water features, and interesting architectural details dotted all around.

The stunning rhododendron and azalea avenue, where hundreds of brilliant blossoms produce a breathtaking display of hues, is one of the garden's attractions. When you visit in the spring, the gardens are painted in a spectrum of pinks, purples, and whites, providing a symphony of blossoms for your viewing pleasure. With more than 150 different types, the gardens also include one of the most impressive collections of camellias in all of Europe.

A trip to Villa Carlotta would not be complete without taking in the views from its expansive terraces. Enjoy breathtaking views of Lake Como, framed by the surrounding Alps, from these elevated vantage points. Give yourself some time to enjoy the peace and quiet and let the breathtaking scenery envelope you.

Villa Carlotta organizes a variety of cultural events and exhibitions all year long, which enhances the experience of visitors even more. These events, which range from art exhibits to classical music performances, revitalize the villa and foster a vibrant culture that embraces the arts in all its manifestations.

16

Como Cathedral

C omo Cathedral, rising magnificently in the center of the city, is a tribute to the rich history of Como as well as the magnificence of Gothic architecture. Known by its formal name, the Cathedral of Santa Maria Assunta, this majestic cathedral is a must-see destination for tourists visiting the charming Lake Como region.

The construction of Como Cathedral took several decades, with additional extensions and modifications afterward. Its foundations date to the late 14th century. The cathedral's design, which honors the Assumption of the Virgin Mary, is a tasteful fusion of Baroque, Renaissance, and Gothic styles. Its well-known façade, with its elaborate features and lovely rose windows, invites people to enter and explore the hidden gems.

The cathedral exudes a sense of breathtaking grandeur and serene spirituality as soon as you walk inside. Natural light streams in through the stained glass windows of the expansive interior, producing an enthralling display of color. Your eyes are drawn upward by the lofty vaulted ceilings, which are decorated with elaborate paintings and elaborate ornaments, inspiring awe and devotion.

The magnificent marble altar, called the Altare Maggiore, is one of the most remarkable aspects of the Como Cathedral. This 18th-century masterwork, which depicts episodes from the life of Christ and the Assumption of the Virgin Mary, was made by local sculptors. It is a symphony of intricate carvings and statues. With its magnificent embellishments that perfectly capture the essence of the Catholic religion, the altar is a real tribute to the talent and workmanship of the artists of the time.

Como Cathedral's Chapel of Sant'Abbondio, honoring the city's patron saint, is another noteworthy feature. The exquisite murals in this elaborate church commemorate Saint Abbondio's life and miracles. Admire the deft brushwork, brilliant colors, and painstaking attention to detail that go into creating these sacred stories. Within the cathedral, the chapel offers a tranquil haven for those seeking peace of mind and comfort from the activity of the outside world.

A unique chance to take in the architectural magnificence of Como Cathedral up close and take in expansive views of the city and Lake Como is provided by ascending the steep stairway to the rooftop decks. This viewpoint allows you to appreciate the cathedral's magnificent presence against the surrounding mountains, as well as its exquisite stone carvings and graceful spires. Make a lasting impression of your stay by taking a moment to appreciate the peace and the amazing views.

The amazing collection of artwork and historical relics may also be seen at Como Cathedral. Richly carved reliquaries, priceless chalices, and liturgical vestments are among the many religious relics kept in the cathedral's treasury. These artifacts demonstrate the significant role the cathedral has played over the ages and provide a window into Como's ecclesiastical and cultural past.

Como Cathedral holds a number of religious events all year long, like as processions and Masses, which give the building an eminently spiritual and devotional atmosphere. A unique chance to see Como's living legacy and feel the enduring faith that permeates the cathedral's walls is offered by attending one of these ceremonies.

Spend some time exploring the quaint Piazza del Duomo sur- rounding Como Cathedral before you end your vacation. This bustling area, which is surrounded by stores, cafes, and ancient buildings, offers a lively environment as well as the opportunity to buy souvenirs or enjoy the local food.

17

Como-Brunate Funicular

T his funicular railway offers a one-of-a-kind experience that blends natural beauty, technical marvels, and
a hint of nostalgia. It connects the city of Como with
the alpine village of Brunate.

One of the oldest funiculars in Italy is the Como-Brunate Funicular, which has been in service since 1894. You are taken back in time to a time when this means of transportation represented the height of contemporary engineering as soon as you board the iconic carriages, which are red and cream in hue. The funicular provides passengers with a smooth and comfortable ride up the high incline. It is made up of two connected carriages that ascend and descend concurrently.

Excitement and eagerness are in the air as the funicular starts to climb. You can see glimpses of Como's quaint streets, lined with quaint homes and old structures, by peering out of the windows. The urban cityscape gives way to a verdant expanse as altitude rises, showcasing the neighboring mountains' natural grandeur and Lake Como's shimmering waters.

But what makes the Como-Brunate Funicular exciting are the expansive views that open out in front of you. The expansive and breathtaking views increase as the funicular ascends higher. Views of the magnificent lake, surrounded by high mountains and quaint settlements scattered along its sides, can be had from the funicular's vantage point.

When you reach Brunate's summit, you emerge onto a crowded plaza with plenty of activities, eateries, and retail establishments. Before beginning a leisurely investigation of this charming community, often known as the "Balcony of the Alps," take time to take in the atmosphere.

The Faro Voltiano, a lighthouse-shaped monument honoring Como-born inventor Alessandro Volta, is one of the highlights of a trip to Brunate. Ascending the monument's steps will reward you with an even more breathtaking all-encompassing vista. Views of Lake Como's sparkling blue waters and an endless range of neighboring mountains are available from this vantage point, which is elevated. It's a breathtaking image that will stay etched in your mind forever.

Brunate is a hiking enthusiast's dream come true, with a plethora of routes winding through the hills and forests all around. Put on your hiking boots and go on a journey where you can experience the peace of nature and find hidden treasures along the route. As you explore Brunate's natural treasures, the sound of rustling leaves, birds tweeting, and fresh mountain air create a calming atmosphere.

For a more relaxed experience, just stroll about the village's enchanting streets, which are lined with vibrant homes, adorable stores, and welcoming cafes. Savor some local specialties or a cup of coffee while admiring Brunate's laid-back atmosphere. When it's time to go down, return to Como via the funicular and enjoy the picturesque ride while reminiscing about the breathtaking scenery you've seen.

Not only is the Como-Brunate Funicular a well-liked tourist destination, but inhabitants also rely on it as a handy means of getting to Brunate, a tranquil haven from the busy city below. It provides a tranquil haven and an opportunity to take in the wonders of nature.

Seize the opportunity to snap pictures of the amazing vistas with your camera or just soak in the beauty around you before riding the Como-Brunate Funicular to the end of your tour. It's an opportunity to consider the engineering wonders of Lake Como and its breathtaking scenery.

18

Gardens of Villa Melzi

The Duke of Lodi and close friend of Napoleon Bonaparte, Francesco Melzi d'Eril, commissioned the construction of the villa and its gardens in the early 1800s, beginning Villa Melzi's history. The mansion itself is a work of architectural art, with neoclassical architecture and tasteful furnishings, frescoes, and columns. But the gardens are what steal the show and win over guests' hearts. There is a sense of peace and natural splendor as soon as you enter the Gardens of

Villa Melzi. The expansive grounds spread out in front of you, beckoning you to take a leisurely walk down the meandering paths and explore the many pleasures that are waiting for you.

The carefully planned gardens have the ideal ratio of wild nature to structured components. Towering trees, meandering streams, and stunning vistas of Lake Como cohabit peacefully with delicate flower beds, well-kept lawns, and precisely placed hedges. Every step leads to an amazing view, and every bend reveals a new surprise—it's a true tribute to the creativity of landscape design.

The breathtaking azalea and rhododendron collection is one of the Gardens of Villa Melzi's attractions. These vivid blooms burst into color in the spring, turning the gardens into an alluring tapestry of pinks, purples, and whites. As you explore, the aroma of the flowers permeates the space, enveloping you in a seductive ambiance.

The lovely Orangerie, a greenhouse that holds a wide variety of exotic plants and tropical species, is another outstanding aspect of the gardens. Enter this enchanted haven and lose yourself in a world of vivid flowers and luxuriant foliage. A peaceful area to enjoy the beauty and diversity of plants from around the globe, the Orangerie provides a much-needed break from the weather.

As you stroll around the Gardens of Villa Melzi, you'll come across architectural features, monuments, and sculptures that enhance the surrounding scenery with a creative touch. Admire the classical statues scattered around the gardens, including the elegant figure of the renowned Italian author Dante Alighieri. These creative pieces complement the surrounding area's overall aesthetic appeal while paying homage to Italy's rich cultural legacy.

The waterfront promenade, with its mesmerizing views of Lake Como and the far-off mountains, is one of the most charming locations in the gardens. Sit down on one of the benches and let the pleasant air and the calming sound of the water falling over you carry you away to a peaceful place. You are left in awe and with greater respect for the surrounding natural treasures by the breathtaking panoramic views that stretch out before you.

Don't forget to visit the quaint cafe inside the grounds as you wrap up your tour of the Gardens of Villa Melzi. Savor the lovely surroundings and the peaceful atmosphere as you treat yourself to a tasty snack or a refreshing drink.

19

Isola Comacina

I sola Comacina is situated close to the hamlet of Ossuccio in the center of Lake Como. The island, which is no more than seven acres in size, offers a singular blend of natural beauty and cultural history. Travelers from all over the world adore it for its beautiful scenery, verdant surroundings, and calm attitude.

Landing on Isola Comacina is like stepping into another planet, where worries from the outer world vanish and time slows down. Cypress and olive trees dot the island's lush terrain, and a plethora of colorful flowers add to the scene's already stunning natural splendor.

The ruins of the old church of San Giovanni Battista are one of the most well-known sights on the island. Once the hub of the island's social and religious life, this church dates back to the eleventh century. The island's rich history and architectural magnificence can still be seen in the remnants, despite having been nearly destroyed in a catastrophic fire in the 19th century.

Discover the mysteries concealed beneath the stone walls of the San Giovanni Battista archeological site and gain insight into the island's past. Explore historic frescoes, elaborate carvings, and the remains of sacred objects that offer insight into the life of the people who formerly called this picturesque location home.

Experiencing the lively food scene of Isola Comacina is one of the attractions of a trip there. There are a few quaint cafes and restaurants on the island where you may enjoy regional specialties and traditional fare. Isola Comacina offers a great gastronomic experience that will satisfy your senses, with dishes ranging from delicious pasta to fresh lake seafood and locally sourced ingredients.

If you want to fully experience Isola Comacina's splendor, stroll around the lovely promenade that encircles the island. With the gorgeous mountains serving as a backdrop, the walk gives breathtaking views of the lake. Choose a quiet area to sit and take in the peace of the surroundings, or just enjoy the sun's warm embrace as it reflects its golden beams onto the blue waters.

Consider going on a boat excursion around Isola Comacina for a different viewpoint. You'll be treated to constantly shifting views of the island's shoreline as you glide over the glistening lake, exposing secret coves, quaint villas, and private beaches. It's a chance to take in the island's splendor from various perspectives and make lifelong memories of your trip.

In addition, Isola Comacina is well-known for its exciting cultural events, especially in the summer. Music performances, art shows, and traditional festivals bring the island to life and highlight the rich cultural legacy of the area. Take part in the celebrations, socialize with the people, and take in the lively vibe of the island.

Isola Comacina is said to be cursed because of its turbulent past and the terrible things that happened here. But the island's eerie beauty and tranquil atmosphere bear witness to its tenacity and timeless allure. It is a spot that captures the hearts of people who visit, leaving an unforgettable impact on their memories.

20

Silk Museum

Museum's Entrance

Nestled within the picturesque city of Como, the Silk Museum stands as a tribute to the city's historical past as a hub of silk manufacturing and workmanship. This intriguing museum provides visitors with a trip through time, highlighting the delicate artistry, technological advancements, and cultural significance of silk manufacturing in Como.

The museum highlights Como's centuries-old link to silk, dating back to the Middle Ages when the city became renowned for its silk manufacturing. Its strategic location on the Silk Road contributed to the flourishing silk trade, making Como a hub for silk manufacture in Europe.

The museum displays the evolution of silk production techniques, from the ancient skill of sericulture to the complicated procedures of silk weaving, dyeing, and printing. Exhibits highlight the technological breakthroughs and artistry that catapulted Como's silk industry to international renown.

Visitors experience a broad collection of exhibits and artifacts that disclose the various stages of silk manufacture. From looms and weaving technology to historical textiles, materials, and samples, these displays offer insights into the artistry and creative delicacy connected with silk making.

The museum celebrates the inventiveness and invention evident in Como's silk industry. Exhibitions showcase the work of designers, artists, and textile producers in developing sophisticated patterns, designs, and silk textiles that received global renown for their quality and beauty.

Silk manufacturing in Como not only contributed to the city's economic development but also played a crucial part in creating its cultural identity. The museum draws attention to the historic significance of silk, showcasing its influence on fashion, art, and trade throughout history.

The Silk Museum offers interactive exhibitions and educational events that captivate visitors of all ages. Interactive exhibits,

workshops, and demonstrations provide a hands-on understanding of silk production techniques, enthralling audiences
and creating an appreciation for the artistry involved.

Dedicated efforts towards conserving the tradition of Como's
silk industry are visible in the museum's conservation programs.
Restoration initiatives assure the maintenance of ancient ma-
chinery, fabrics, and artifacts, protecting these treasures for
future generations.

The museum serves as a platform for community participation,
providing cultural events, exhibitions, and workshops that highlight the art of silk. These events promote cultural interaction,
display current silk works, and cultivate a sense of pride in
Como's silk legacy.

The Silk Museum also actively collaborates with educational
institutions, delivering tailor-made programs and educational
outreach activities. These programs aim to educate students
and tourists about the history, technology, and craftsmanship
related to silk manufacture.

21

Orrido di Bellano

O rrido di Bellano is a tribute to the force of nature's sculpting prowess. The valley, sculpted by the rushing waters of the Pioverna River over thousands of years, displays towering limestone cliffs rising sharply on each side. The chiseling force of the river has produced a captivating maze of tunnels, caverns, and gaps, enticing exploration and astonishment.

The gorge's steep terrain is accented by flowing waterfalls that provide a sense of peacefulness and vitality to the area.

The sound of rushing water echoes within the gorge, intensifying the realistic experience. Visitors can watch the interplay of light and shadow on the stone walls, producing a captivating spectacle.

The centerpiece of Orrido di Bellano is the suspension bridge that spans the canyon, offering tourists a thrilling vantage point to admire the natural beauty below. The bridge offers panoramic views of falling streams, towering cliffs, and rich flora, making it a photographer's dream and a location to immerse oneself in the grandeur of the surroundings.

The gorge is covered with a magnificent tapestry of flora and wildlife, living in the microclimate provided by the limestone walls. Mosses, ferns, and other flora cling to the rocks, forming a verdant tapestry amidst the rough environment. The diversified ecosystem supports many bird species and small creatures, contributing to the attractiveness of the natural surroundings.

Beyond its natural grandeur, Orrido di Bellano possesses historical value. The location was employed in the past for its hydraulic ability to power nearby mills. The relics of these ancient structures stand as a testimony to the area's industrial past, bringing an extra element of historical intrigue to the gorge.

Visitors to Orrido di Bellano can go on guided tours or self-directed explorations, allowing them to navigate the network of trails that wind through the canyon. The entire experience allows an opportunity to appreciate the geological formations up close, witness the strength of the river, and revel in the calm of the natural surroundings.

The gorge's peculiarity extends to its educational significance. An interpretive center offers insights into the geological processes that produced the gorge, giving an enriching experience for visitors interested in comprehending the natural forces at play.

22

Forte Montecchio Nord

L ocated near Colico on Lake Como's northern shoreline, Forte Montecchio Nord stands as an enduring
emblem of military might and strategic significance.
Constructed in the early 20th century, this castle was part of a
network of defensive structures created during World War I to
secure the Alpine region. Its strategic posture enabled control
over critical passageways, serving as a key element in securing
the surrounding areas.

The fortress's architectural design embodies a mix of sturdy concrete walls and intricate underground passageways. Its elaborate network of bunkers, artillery installations, and interconnecting passages beautifully merges with the natural landscape, showing the skill and elegance of military architecture during that era.

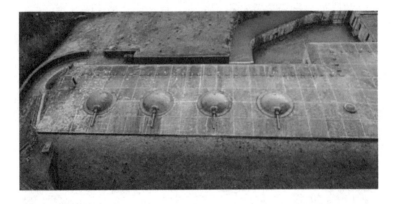

During World War I, Forte Montecchio Nord played a key role in defending the region, functioning as a barrier against potential invaders. Its strategic location and firepower made it an essential component in the defensive strategy of the area, highlighting its historical significance in shaping the outcomes of past conflicts.

The fortress houses a remarkable collection of well-preserved artillery pieces and weaponry, providing visitors with a glimpse into the technological advancements and firepower employed during its active service. These exhibitions realistically represent the equipment and lifestyle of the troops who were stationed within the fortress walls.

Visitors have the chance to join in guided tours that offer a full understanding of the fortress's history, architectural subtleties, and military strategies used during its operating period. Traversing the underground hallways and chambers, travelers receive insights into the obstacles faced by soldiers and the fortress's essential role in ancient combat.

Perched on an elevated position, Forte Montecchio Nord offers stunning panoramic views of Lake Como, the surrounding mountains, and the lovely surroundings. The juxtaposition of the fortress's strong structure against the calm beauty of its natural surroundings produces a fascinating ambiance, inviting visitors to appreciate both its historical significance and the gorgeous scenery.

Dedicated efforts toward conservation and restoration assure the preservation of the fortress's historical legacy and architectural authenticity. Ongoing projects aim to protect the structural integrity of the stronghold while enabling tourists to access and understand its historical significance.

The stronghold organizes periodic cultural events, exhibitions, and historical reenactments that pay tribute to its military legacy. These activities serve as participatory platforms, allowing visitors to immerse themselves in historical circumstances and obtain a fuller understanding of life within the stronghold during conflict.

Forte Montecchio Nord acts as an educational resource, conducting instructional programs and workshops for schools and institutions. These programs aim to emphasize the fortress's historical, architectural, and military importance, increasing community interaction and promoting the preservation of cultural assets.

23

Basilica Di San Giacomo

Nestled within the lovely city of Bellagio on the shores of Lake Como, the Basilica Di San Giacomo stands as an epitome of spiritual devotion, architectural magnificence, and cultural legacy. This beautiful basilica, steeped in history and filled with exquisite artwork, captivates tourists with its religious significance and appealing style.

Dating back to the 12th century, Basilica Di San Giacomo serves as a witness to centuries of religious devotion. Dedicated to Saint James (Giacomo), the patron saint of travelers and pilgrims, the basilica has been a destination of worship and pilgrimage, attracting ardent worshippers and visitors seeking spiritual peace.

The basilica's architectural design shows a harmonious blend of Romanesque, Gothic, and Renaissance influences, illustrating the growth of architectural styles over several epochs. Its exterior, embellished with elaborate sculptures and rich ornamentation, conveys ageless beauty and craftsmanship.

Stepping into Basilica Di San Giacomo shows a sanctuary decorated with gorgeous murals, delicate woodwork, and stunning altars that relate biblical events and religious symbols. The interplay of light streaming through stained glass windows enriches the ambiance, enriching the spiritual experience for worshippers and tourists alike.

The basilica houses a collection of religious relics, including sacred artifacts and historical treasures. These artifacts offer a glimpse into the religious practices and cultural heritage of the region, adding depth to the basilica's historical significance.

Beyond its architectural splendor, Basilica Di San Giacomo serves as a focal point for the local community, hosting religious ceremonies, celebrations, and cultural events. These events foster a sense of communal unity and spiritual nourishment among worshippers and visitors.

Dedicated efforts towards conservation and restoration ensure the preservation of Basilica Di San Giacomo's architectural integrity and historical value. Restoration initiatives strive to safeguard the artwork, structural stability, and cultural heritage for future generations to admire.

Occasional creative events, concerts, and cultural festivals held within the basilica pay tribute to its religious and historical history. These activities complement the visiting experience, giving a forum for artistic expression and remembering the basilica's cultural past.

The basilica engages in educational outreach, offering programs and projects for students and visitors to learn about its religious and cultural significance. These educational activities strive to instill an appreciation for religious tradition and enhance cultural understanding.

24

Accommodation Recommendations

S electing the ideal lodging for your Lake Como vacation is another crucial choice that can significantly improve your entire experience. There are numerous lodging choices available in Lake Como to accommodate a range of tastes, spending limits, and vacation styles. This chapter will walk you through the variety of lodging possibilities in the area, from opulent hotels to little bed & breakfasts.

Hotels

There is a wide range of hotels in Lake Como to suit the needs of different types of visitors. Nestled around the beaches are luxurious resorts and five-star hotels that provide amazing views of the lake, luxurious amenities, and first-rate service. High levels of comfort are offered by these institutions, which frequently have fine dining restaurants, spas, swimming pools, and well-appointed rooms and suites.

Here we'll be looking at some very good 5-star hotels and luxurious resorts you can choose to lay your head on while you're in Lake Como.

1. **Grand Hotel Tremezzo**: Perched above Lake Como, this opulent Art Nouveau establishment stands 250 meters away from the renowned Villa Carlotta museum and botanical gardens.

The refined accommodations feature modern amenities like Wi-Fi, flat-screen TVs, minibars, and scenic park or lake vistas. Select rooms boast balconies or cozy sitting areas. Suites offer luxurious whirlpool tubs, with some featuring private gardens. For an elevated experience, rooftop suites come with dedicated butlers and terraces equipped with hot tubs, while room service caters to guests' needs.

Guests can indulge in a delightful breakfast served at an upscale restaurant with a terrace, alongside a laid-back trattoria, an upscale bar, a beachfront bistro, and a casual pizzeria by the pool. The hotel boasts an array of amenities, including three pools, a private beach, and a marina. Additionally, a spa, fitness room, and tennis court cater to guests seeking relaxation or activities during their stay. For more inquiries/booking, contact the hotel at +39 0344 42491.

2. **Palace hotel**: Situated just moments away from the shores of Lake Como, this majestic hotel, housed within a meticulously restored Art Nouveau palace, stands merely a minute's stroll from Lake Como. Conveniently positioned, it's a brief three-minute walk from Como Lago train station and a five-minute walk from the impressive Cathedral of Como.

The elegantly appointed rooms feature modern amenities such as Wi-Fi, flat-screen TVs, desks, and minibars, with some offering charming balconies. For an enhanced experience, upgraded rooms showcase picturesque vistas of Lake Como, while suites boast spacious separate living areas. Guests can also enjoy the convenience of room service during their stay.

Within the hotel, guests will find an opulent ballroom, a sophisticated restaurant that provides captivating views of the lake, and a charming bar nestled in a glass conservatory, perfect for enjoying sunset vistas. Additionally, breakfast options and parking facilities are available to guests during their stay. For more inquiries dial +39 031 23391.

3. Hilton Lake Como

Nestled alongside the picturesque shores of Lake Como, the Hilton Lake Como stands as an elegant accommodation option, conveniently located just 1 kilometer away from both the Como San Giovanni train station and the charming Villa Olmo, renowned for its 18th-century architecture and stunning lakeside gardens.

The well-appointed rooms boast an abundance of natural light streaming through their floor-to-ceiling windows, equipped with modern amenities such as flat-screen TVs, minibars, and facilities for brewing tea and coffee. For those seeking an elevated experience, upgraded rooms showcase breathtaking views of the lake and may feature comfortable sofa beds. Moreover, the suites offer spacious living areas, balcony hot tubs, and in some cases, bi-level layouts for added comfort. Guests can stay connected with Wi-Fi and enjoy round-the-clock room service.

This hotel doesn't fall short on indulgence, offering an array of amenities including two dining options and a rooftop terrace featuring an infinity pool, a hot tub, a bar, and panoramic views of the lake. Additionally, an indoor pool, a rejuvenating spa, and a well-equipped gym cater to guests' relaxation and fitness needs. Guests can opt for a fee-based package that includes breakfast and parking, and the hotel warmly welcomes pets. For more inquiries dial +39 031 338 2611.

4. **Hotel Barchetta Excelsior**: Positioned overlooking the charming Piazza Cavour on the tranquil shores of Lago di Como, this refined hotel offers an upscale experience. It's conveniently situated just a four-minute walk from Teatro Sociale and a brief 10-minute stroll from the Como S. Giovanni train station.

The comfortable rooms offer complimentary Wi-Fi, flat-screen TVs, and minibars, with some boasting serene lake views or inviting balconies. Upgraded rooms and suites include additional amenities such as tea and coffeemakers, while suites also feature spacious living areas. Guests can also avail themselves of room service during their stay.

The hotel provides a complimentary breakfast buffet, allowing guests to start their day on a delightful note. Further enhancing the experience, guests can enjoy dining at a restaurant offering captivating views of the lake, a relaxed bistro, and a cozy bar within the premises. Additionally, parking facilities are available at a nearby sister hotel for a fee. To contact the hotel for further inquiries, dial +39 031 3221.

5. **Vista Lago di Como:** Positioned just a stone's throw from the captivating shores of Lake Como, this upscale hotel offers a high-end experience and enjoys a prime location within a

five-minute stroll from both Lago Como train station and Como Cathedral.

Characterized by plush fabrics and exquisite antique furnishings, the rooms exude sophistication and are equipped with modern conveniences such as Wi-Fi, flat-screen TVs, minibars, and tea/coffeemakers. Suites boast separate living areas, and the majority of accommodations treat guests to breathtaking views of the lake. For added luxury, room service includes the option of a personal chef.

Guests can indulge in breakfast offerings available on-site. Additionally, the hotel boasts an elegant rooftop terrace hosting an upscale restaurant and a bar, providing a scenic backdrop. Adventure-seekers can take advantage of seaplane and motor-boat tours or explore the area with bike rentals offered by the hotel. For more inquiries/booking dial +39 031 537 5241.

6. **Passalacqua**: Situated in Moltrasio, merely 6.3 kilometers from Villa Olmo, Passalacqua presents accommodation that includes an outdoor swimming pool, complimentary private parking, a fitness center, and a beautifully landscaped garden. The property boasts a restaurant, a shared lounge area, as well as conveniences like a sauna and a hammam. Guests can also access shared kitchen facilities, room service, and currency exchange during their stay.

The hotel offers air-conditioned rooms equipped with amenities such as a wardrobe, coffee machine, minibar, safety deposit box, flat-screen TV, and a private bathroom featuring a bidet. Certain units at Passalacqua showcase picturesque lake views, while all rooms include a kettle for added convenience.

Guests can enjoy a continental, Italian, or American breakfast served each morning at the property. Additionally, the accommodation provides a luxurious 5-star experience, including access to a spa center and a terrace. For recreational activities, guests have the opportunity to play tennis on-site and can also opt for bike rentals available at Passalacqua. For more inquiries dial +039 031 44311.

More Affordable Options

For those seeking a more affordable option, three-star hotels, and other smaller ones can be found in various towns around the lake.

1. **Hotel Florence:**
   Situated along the picturesque Lake Como, Hotel Florence offers an ideal location, just 3.1 km away from the renowned Villa Carlotta art museum and botanic gardens, and a mere 8 km from the captivating Birds of Prey Center at Castello di Vezio.

The hotel boasts vibrant rooms and suites adorned with classic, old-world furnishings. Guests can enjoy complimentary Wi-Fi, along with the luxury of 4-poster beds and balconies or terraces that offer breathtaking views of the lake.

A delightful breakfast buffet is included, complemented by a charming restaurant adorned with arched ceilings and an inviting lakeside terrace shaded by trees, perfect for outdoor dining. Moreover, the wood-paneled bar, complete with an outdoor area, exudes a cozy ambiance. For relaxation, the hotel features an upscale spa and a welcoming lounge. For more information, you can contact the hotel by dialing +39 031 950342.

2. **B&B Hotel Como**: Situated in Como, just 550 meters away from Como Nord Camerlata Train Station, B&B Hotel Como offers complimentary WiFi throughout the premises.

The contemporary rooms feature air conditioning, a safe, and a satellite TV. Additionally, each room boasts a private bathroom equipped with a shower and a hairdryer.

Exploring the nearby attractions is convenient, with Piazza Cavour Square and the stunning Lake Como both just a 10-minute drive from the hotel's location. For more inquiries dial +39 031 260485

3. **Borgovico Hotel**:
Nestled in a 19th-century stone building, Borgovico Hotel is a relaxed retreat located just a minute's stroll from the nearest bus stop. The hotel is conveniently positioned at a distance of 1 km from both the Teatro Sociale Theater and Como Cathedral.

Each uniquely adorned room offers complimentary Wi-Fi, flat-screen TVs, desks, and cozy sitting areas, ensuring a comfortable stay. Guests can also enjoy room service during their visit.

In the vibrant dining area, guests can indulge in a breakfast buffet (at an additional cost) before exploring the city. The hotel features a laid-back bar and a charming courtyard with seating, providing serene spaces to unwind. With prior notice, pets are welcomed at no charge for select animals. For more inquiries dial +39 031 570107.

4. Hotel La Perla:

Nestled within a 19th-century stone building, the relaxed Borgovico Hotel is conveniently a minute's stroll from the nearest bus stop and approximately 1 km away from both the Teatro Sociale theater and the Como Cathedral.

The individually decorated rooms, offering complimentary Wi-Fi, feature flat-screen TVs, desks, and cozy sitting areas. Guests can also enjoy room service during their stay.

Start the day with a breakfast buffet served in a vibrant dining area. Additionally, guests can unwind in the low-key bar or relax in the courtyard's seating area. Pets are welcome upon prior notice, with some animals staying free of charge. You can contact the hotel by dialing +39 0344 41707.

5. Hotel Montecodeno:

Montecodeno, a laid-back hotel located in the town center, is just a 4-minute stroll from the Varenna Esino train station. Additionally, it's conveniently situated within a 10-minute walk from Villa Monastero and only 2 minutes from the shores of Lake Como.

The warmly decorated rooms offer complimentary Wi-Fi and flat-screen TVs. For added comfort, upgraded rooms feature cozy sitting areas.

Guests can enjoy a free breakfast buffet during their stay. The hotel provides a charming bar and a relaxed restaurant offering terrace dining, along with a pleasant garden area for guests to unwind. For more information dial +39 0341 830123.

5. **Villa Belvedere Como Lake Relais:**

Situated along the SS 340, approximately 21 km away from Como, Villa Belvedere Como Lake Relais is an elegant hotel resting on the shores of Lake Como, just 5 km from Isola Comacina.

The hotel offers simple yet refined rooms equipped with complimentary Wi-Fi and satellite TV. Upgraded rooms boast balconies, terraces, and lake views, while some include minibars. Suites feature separate living areas with pull-out sofas, and guests can also opt for room service.

Guests can enjoy complimentary parking and a continental breakfast buffet. The hotel boasts a sophisticated restaurant with a terrace showcasing stunning lake views. Additionally, there's a cozy bar and a business center available for guests' convenience. For more information dial +39 031 821 1116.

6. **Hotel Tre Re:** Hotel Tre Re, an unassuming hotel set within a former convent, is conveniently located within a brief 5-minute stroll from Lake Como, the Teatro Sociale opera house, and the Cattedrale di Santa Maria Assunta.

The rooms and suites, modestly furnished, feature amenities

such as desks, flat-screen TVs, and complimentary Wi-Fi access.

Guests can enjoy complimentary breakfast and parking during their stay. The hotel boasts a luminous restaurant adorned with high ceilings as well as a bar for guests' convenience. For more information dial +39 031 265374.

7. **Posta Design Hotel**: Set on Piazza Alessandro Volta, Posta Design Hotel occupies an elegant boutique space within a rationalist building crafted by architect Giuseppe Terragni. This upscale hotel is conveniently situated just a 5-minute stroll from the medieval Como Cathedral.

The hotel offers sleek rooms featuring marble bathrooms, flat-screen TVs, safes, and complimentary Wi-Fi. Some upgraded rooms offer delightful views of the piazza, while an airy suite boasts a terrace and a skylight.

Guests can enjoy the ambiance of a chic bistro and a bar within the hotel premises. Additionally, breakfast is available to start the day off right. For more inquiries dial +39 031 276 9011.

8. **Lizard Hotel:**
Lizard Hotel, located close to the historic city center, is conveniently positioned within a 5-minute walk from two bus stops. Additionally, it's a mere 12-minute stroll from the Basilica of Sant'Abbondio and approximately 2 km away from Teatro Sociale.

The hotel offers bright and modestly furnished rooms equipped with Wi-Fi, flat-screen TVs, desks, sitting areas, and minibars. Guests can also enjoy the convenience of room service.

Start your day with breakfast offered at the hotel. Lizard Hotel features a charming restaurant, a casual bar, a gym, and a furnished terrace for guests' relaxation. Furthermore, guests can indulge in amenities such as a sauna and a hammam. Parking facilities are also available for guests' convenience. For more information dial +39 031 403 8102.

9. **Hotel Marco's**: Hotel Marco's, situated just across from a lake promenade, offers a relaxed setting. It's conveniently positioned a minute's walk from the Como-Brunate funicular and a brief 10-minute stroll from Como Cathedral.

The hotel features airy and modestly furnished rooms with marble or tiled floors, equipped with flat-screen TVs, Wi-Fi, desks, and minibars. For added comfort, upgraded rooms offer delightful lake views and/or balconies. Guests can also avail themselves of room service during their stay.

Enjoy breakfast served either in a dining room or on a terrace that offers picturesque views of the lake. Additionally, the hotel boasts a pizzeria equipped with a wood-burning oven and a bar for guests' convenience. Parking facilities are also available. For more information dial +39 031 303 628.

10. **Hotel Quarcino**:

Hotel Quarcino, with a serene view of Lake Como, offers a laid-back setting just a 3-minute walk from Como Lago train station and approximately 3 km from the beautifully landscaped gardens at Villa Olmo dating back to the 18th century.

The hotel presents casual and modestly furnished rooms featuring parquet floors, equipped with complimentary Wi-Fi, flat-screen TVs, desks, and minibars. Upgraded room options include balconies and/or delightful views of the lake.

Guests can benefit from complimentary parking and enjoy the hotel's garden area. Start your day with a breakfast buffet, and pets are also warmly welcomed at the hotel. For more information dial +39 031 303934.

11. **Palazzo Albricci Peregrine**:
Situated in Como, Palazzo Albricci Peregrini features various amenities including free bikes, a bar, a shared lounge, and a garden. The property offers a concierge service, luggage storage, and complimentary WiFi accessible throughout. It's conveniently located just 500 meters from Broletto.

The rooms at this establishment are equipped with air conditioning, a flat-screen TV with satellite channels, a kettle, a bidet, a hairdryer, and a wardrobe. Additionally, each room boasts a private bathroom with a shower, free toiletries, and a pleasant garden view.

Guests at Palazzo Albricci Peregrini can enjoy either a continental or buffet breakfast during their stay. For more inquiries dial +39 331 230 5764.

Bed and Breakfasts/Guesthouses

For those looking for a more individualized and private encounter, bed and breakfasts, or B&Bs, are a popular option. Several little B&Bs in Lake Como provide warm, inviting lodging in a lovely setting. These lodging options are usually family-run businesses that will make your stay more enjoyable with a kind greeting and local knowledge. Fresh, locally sourced breakfasts are frequently served at B&Bs, ensuring a great start to the day. Let's look at some great options you can choose from below;

1. **Fio & Gio:** Fiò & Giò, situated in Varenna center, is just a one-minute stroll from the serene shores of Lake Como, providing complimentary Wi-Fi and an inviting terrace offering scenic views of the lake.

The rooms are furnished with a TV, a safety deposit box, and a work desk. Each room shares a well-equipped bathroom with complimentary toiletries.

Guests can enjoy a daily Italian breakfast inclusive of a hot drink and croissant, served at the bar only 20 meters away from the property.

For those looking to explore, the ferries to Bellagio are conveniently within a 10-minute walk from Fiò & Giò, while the Medieval Castle of Vezio stands at a distance of 3 km. You can contact the Bed and Breakfast by dialing +39 031 821116.

2. **BB La Magnolia**: B&B Magnolia provides guests with soundproofed rooms that include complimentary Wi-Fi and a private

bathroom. This charming accommodation also offers a private garden and a cozy TV lounge featuring a fireplace. Upon reservation, guests can avail themselves of a free parking space.

Start your day with a delightful sweet or savory breakfast at a nearby café. The rooms are equipped with cooling fans and furnished with elegant wrought-iron beds.

Conveniently situated just 300 meters from central Sulmona, guests can easily explore the town's main attractions such as Sulmona Cathedral and Garibaldi Square within a short 3-minute walk. The nearest bus stop is a mere 200 meters away from the property. For more information dial the establishment at +39 349 462 0733.

3. La Tana Rooms:

Nestled in Lenno, just 700 meters away from Villa Balbianello, La Tana Rooms offers accommodation with a garden, private parking, and a terrace. The air-conditioned rooms boast a serene garden view, featuring a desk and complimentary WiFi.

Each room at the guest house is equipped with a wardrobe, a flat-screen TV, and a private bathroom for guests' convenience.

Start your day with a buffet breakfast served daily at La Tana Rooms. For more information dial +39 346 673 1832.

4. Santagata Bed & Breakfast: SantAgata Bed and Breakfast offers a picturesque setting with a garden and garden views, situated just 400 meters from Como Borghi Train Station. Throughout the property, guests can enjoy free WiFi, and

convenient private parking is available on-site. Moreover, the guest house provides facilities catering to disabled guests.

The air-conditioned units at this guest house are well-equipped, featuring amenities such as a desk, kettle, minibar, safety deposit box, flat-screen TV, and a private bathroom with a walk-in shower. Some units boast terraces or balconies offering stunning mountain views and outdoor furniture. Guests can expect bed linen and towels provided during their stay.

Each morning, guests can indulge in a variety of breakfast options, including Continental and Italian specialties, alongside fresh pastries, fruits, and local delights. The guest house also houses a coffee shop and a convenient minimarket.

For relaxation, guests can unwind in the shared lounge area provided.

SantAgata Bed and Breakfast enjoys a prime location near several notable attractions including Como Cathedral, making it an ideal stay for exploring the area. For more inquiries dial +39 339 528 5589.

5. **Le Stanze del Lago**: Le Stanze del Lago Suites & Pool in Como offers exclusive accommodation for adults, featuring amenities such as an open-air bath, a serene garden, and a shared lounge. The property provides convenient private parking on-site. Guests can relax on the sun terrace, take a dip in the seasonal outdoor pool, or enjoy views of the city and the inner courtyard.

All accommodations are equipped with air conditioning and flat-screen TVs. Each unit includes a kettle, a private bathroom, and complimentary WiFi. Some rooms offer balconies or pool views. Guests can expect bed linen and towels provided during their stay.

The guest house serves a varied breakfast, including local specialties, fresh pastries, and fruits. Additionally, room service for breakfast is available. For those planning day trips, the guest house offers packed lunches.

Le Stanze del Lago boasts various wellness amenities, including a fitness room, a solarium, and yoga classes. Guests can also take advantage of the bicycle rental service provided by Le Stanze del Lago Suites & Pool. For more inquiries dial +39 339 544 6515.

6. **Essentia Guesthouse**: Nestled atop a wooded hill with stunning views of Lake Como, Essentia Guesthouse offers an elegant retreat, located 12 km away from Como Lago train station and approximately 13 km from Como Cathedral.

The guesthouse offers country-style rooms featuring complimentary Wi-Fi, flat-screen TVs, and fireplaces, accompanied by tea and coffeemakers. One room provides picturesque views of the lake. Additionally, a suite includes a separate living area, while all rooms boast en suite bathrooms.

Guests can unwind in the garden area, which features a relaxing hot tub. The guesthouse offers breakfast and evening meals for an additional fee, served in a glass-enclosed dining room that showcases breathtaking views of the lake. For more information dial +39 327 732 6920.

7. **Rumi Rooms:** Rumi Rooms, a historic establishment, sits just 700 meters from the Como San Giovanni Train Station. This property offers free WiFi and features a bar. Guests can enjoy the convenience of private check-in and check-out, along with access to a family-friendly restaurant. The guest house provides family rooms for guests' comfort.

At Rumi Rooms, guests can expect air-conditioned units furnished with a desk, kettle, minibar, safety deposit box, flat-screen TV, and a private bathroom equipped with a bidet. All units feature a private entrance and include a wardrobe for added convenience.

Points of interest nearby include the Volta Temple, Basilica of Sant'Abbondio, and Como Borghi Train Station, making Rumi Rooms an ideal location for exploring the city's attractions. For more information dial +39 031 207 2356.

8. **Lakeviewcabin:** Lakeviewcabin, a property featuring a garden and terrace, is located in Como, conveniently situated not too far away from Villa Olmo and the Volta Temple. The bed and breakfast offers rooms equipped with air conditioning, complimentary private parking, and free WiFi.

Guest rooms at the bed and breakfast include amenities such as a flat-screen TV and a private bathroom featuring a hairdryer, free toiletries, and a shower. Each unit is provided with bed linen and towels.

For travelers' convenience, the nearest airport, Milan Malpensa, is 52 km away from Lakeviewcabin. The property also offers a paid airport shuttle service. For more inquiries dial +39 331 258 0962.

Agriturismo

Agriturismo, which combines the Italian terms for "agriculture" and "tourism," is a different kind of lodging that lets guests enjoy Lake Como's rural and agricultural features. Working farms that provide lodging for guests are frequently known as agriturismo enterprises. An agriturismo offers a special setting for experiencing nature, sampling regional food, and learning about customary farming methods. These lodging options include both remodeled farmhouses and rustic cottages; some even provide farm-to-table meals. Let's look at some good options below:

1. **Cà Del Lago:** Ca de lago is a rural farmstay located on a working farm, just a 9-minute walk away from the scenic shores of Lake Como.

The simple rooms at this farm stay boast wood floors and traditional country-style decor. Each room offers amenities such as Wi-Fi and satellite TV. Depending on the room type, guests may enjoy additional features like views of the mountains or the lake, private terraces, or cozy fireplaces.

Guests can dine in an airy restaurant showcasing floor-to-ceiling windows, exposed stone walls, and a charming wood ceiling. The property also offers a spa area, which includes a hot tub, sauna, and Turkish bath. Additionally, there's an outdoor pool equipped with comfortable sun loungers and a playground for added recreation. Guests can start their day with a breakfast buffet at the farm stay. For more inquiries dial +39 0344 82735.

2. C'era una Volta B&B:

C'era Una Volta B&B is situated in the serene countryside near Perugia, offering air-conditioned rooms, complimentary Wi-Fi throughout the property, and free private parking.

The rooms are adorned with a classic décor and feature amenities such as a TV, as well as an en suite bathroom equipped with complimentary toiletries and a hairdryer.

Guests at C'era Una Volta B&B can kickstart their day with a delightful breakfast comprising sweet biscuits, cereal, and homemade cakes. Upon request, the B&B also offers gluten-free options for guests with dietary preferences. For more inquiries dial +39 0341 815070.

3. Agriturismo Crotto di Somana:

Nestled in the countryside of Mandello del Lario, Agriturismo Crotto Di Somana presents rustic-style accommodation with a garden and a dedicated wellness area. This property offers picturesque views of Lake Como and the neighboring mountains, along with convenient BBQ facilities.

Featuring complimentary Wi-Fi and air conditioning, all rooms at the agriturismo boast a flat-screen TV and a private entrance. The en suite bathrooms are equipped with showers for guests' comfort.

Agriturismo Crotto Di Somana operates using solar panels for its power supply, promoting sustainable living.

Guests can enjoy a continental breakfast served daily in the kitchen area, providing a comforting start to the day amidst the serene countryside. For more information dial +39 338 451 9777.

Location Consideration

Take your tastes and the activities you intend to partake in into account when selecting your lodging. Seek lodging in smaller towns or villages away from the busy tourist areas if you want a quiet and private stay. Staying in a larger town like Como, Bellagio, or Varenna, will give you quick access to restaurants, shops, and activities if you want a bustling atmosphere. Lakefront lodging also provides breathtaking vistas and convenient access to water sports.

Booking Recommendations: Because Lake Como is a well-liked tourist attraction, it is best to reserve your lodging in advance, particularly during the busiest travel periods. Making reservations in advance guarantees that you'll have more options and can get the best prices. Numerous online travel agencies and hotel booking websites offer a wide selection of lodging choices in Lake Como, making it simple for you to compare costs, read reviews, and make bookings.

Take into account the facilities and services provided by the lodging before confirming your reservation. Ascertain whether you need any particular amenities, like air conditioning, Wi-Fi, parking, or a pool. For example, if you would prefer a room with a balcony or a view of the lake, it is recommended to get in touch with the hotel directly to check on availability.

Reading reviews from prior visitors can also help gain knowledge about the level of cleanliness, service, and general experience at a specific lodging. You can get useful information from these reviews and use it to guide your decision-making.

Finally, when choosing your lodging, don't forget to take your budget into account. Every price range can find something to suit their needs at Lake Como, from luxurious resorts to reasonably priced bed and breakfasts or campers. Sort your demands based on priority and decide how much you are willing to spend on lodging.

IV

Enjoy The Culture

25

Food and Dining

Not only does Lake Como enthrall tourists with its gorgeous scenery and quaint towns, but its mouthwatering food also stimulates the senses. Lake Como, which is tucked away in the heart of Italy's Lombardy region, is known for its abundant lake and the tastes of its surroundings. This chapter extends an invitation for you to take a culinary tour and explore the delicious food and dining establishments in this charming area.

The cuisine of Lake Como is a tasteful fusion of regional delicacies influenced by the surrounding area and classic Italian fare. There is something to please every pallet, from sumptuous meats and fresh lake fish to delicious pasta.

Risotto is one of Lake Como's signature meals. The region is renowned for its variants of this creamy rice dish, which is a true culinary wonder. One of the most well-liked is risotto alla milanese, a rich and aromatic risotto flavored with saffron. Other local delicacies include risotto with perch, which highlights the region's seasonal products, and risotto with asparagus, which combines the subtle flavors of the lake fish with the creamy rice.

Lake Como provides a delicious variety of pasta options. Savor the classic pizzoccheri dish, which consists of buckwheat pasta topped with melted cheese, potatoes, and cabbage. For those looking for comfort cuisine with a regional twist, this filling and substantial dish is a great option. Another specialty of pasta is cancelli, which is stuffed pasta with a filling that is distinct from ravioli in both shape and style. Usually served with butter and sage, these bite-sized treats are stuffed with a blend of meat, breadcrumbs, and regional cheese.

Because of its proximity to Lake Como, fresh fish is a staple of the local cuisine. Try the lavarello, a mild whitefish that is only found in Lake Como. This fish is typically served grilled or with a light sauce so that its inherent qualities can be fully appreciated. Missoltini, which are small lake fish that are salted, dried, and then grilled or fried, and pan-fried to perfection perch fillets served with a squeeze of lemon are two more classic fish dishes.

A trip to Lake Como wouldn't be complete without sampling some of the area's well-known cheeses. Superior cheeses are produced all over the Lombardy region, and Lake Como is no different. Savor the delightfully creamy richness of Taleggio, a mildly acidic cheese that goes well with regional wines. Bitto is a semi-hard cheese that has been aged for at least 70 months and has a hint of nutty flavor. It is worth trying. These cheeses lend a rich and unique flavor to many recipes and are frequently included on regional cheese boards.

Lake Como offers an array of wines to pair with your dinner. Excellent reds, whites, and sparkling wines are produced in the area, which is well-known for them. Enjoy a crisp and refreshing glass of white wine, such as the fragrant Terrazze Retiche di Sondrio, or sip on a bottle of the local red wine, Valtellina, which is produced from the Nebbiolo vine. Not to be overlooked is the delightful Franciacorta sparkling wine, which is made in the nearby Lombardy region.

There's more to eat in Lake Como than just classic restaurants. Many quaint osterias and trattorias in the area provide genuine, small-plate eating experiences. These neighborhood restaurants frequently serve family recipes that have been handed down over the years, capturing the authentic flavor of Lake Como food. In these undiscovered culinary jewels, enjoy hearty meals prepared with passion and attention to detail, strike up vibrant conversations with the welcoming locals, and make enduring memories.

Some Michelin-starred restaurants around Lake Como offer cutting-edge culinary delights for customers looking for a more upscale dining experience. These restaurants offer a gourmet adventure that blends regional products with cutting-edge preparation methods, pushing the limits of taste and presentation. Savor carefully prepared foods that are a visual feast as well as a palate-pleasing experience.

Take a cooking class or go on a food tour to experience Lake Como's gastronomic culture. These experiences offer the chance to pick the brains of regional chefs, unearth the mysteries of time-honored recipes, and prepare real food with your hands. Explore nearby marketplaces, select the freshest ingredients, and work with skilled chefs to turn them into culinary masterpieces. It's an opportunity to learn more about Lake Como's food and take a little piece of Italy home with you.

Finally, don't forget to indulge in Lake Como's delicious desserts to sate your sweet craving. Try the miascia, a classic cake composed of almonds, dried fruits, and wine-soaked bread that is a local specialty. Savor the velvety richness of tiramisu, an age-old Italian dessert that never lets you down. Naturally, a trip to Italy wouldn't be complete without trying gelato. Enjoy a scoop—or two—of this velvety, creamy frozen treat, which comes in a range of flavors to satisfy any palate.

Suggested eateries and coffee shops

There are several eateries and cafés in Lake Como that offer the best local and Italian cuisines. Every taste may be satisfied at Lake Como, from sophisticated restaurants offering creative culinary concoctions to classic trattorias serving handcrafted delicacies. This chapter features a list of suggested eateries and cafés that will undoubtedly make your trip to Lake Como's cuisine unforgettable.

1. **La Punta**: Tucked away in the quaint village of Bellagio, La Punta is renowned for its mouthwatering food and breathtaking views of the lake. This cozy, family-run eatery specializes in classic Italian cuisine and has a friendly, inviting ambiance. Savor delectable pasta meals, fresh seafood, and decadent desserts while taking in expansive views of Lake Como from the outdoor patio.

2. **Osteria Antica Molina**: This classic trattoria, hidden away in the village of Molina, embodies the spirit of Lake Como's gastronomic legacy. An attractive and cozy ambiance is created by the restaurant's hearty meals, courteous service, and rustic charm. Taste authentic regional cuisine, made with passion and locally obtained ingredients, like pizzoccheri, polenta, and cheeses. Don't pass up the chance to complement your dinner with a bottle from their large wine list, which includes both Italian and local favorites.

3. **Ristorante Il Gatto Nero**: This restaurant, which is located in Cernobbio, is well-known for its superb food and sophisticated atmosphere. With a focus on using seasonal foods, the menu at this Michelin-starred restaurant showcases regional characteristics. Every meal, from flavorful meats to inventive vegetarian selections, is expertly cooked and elegantly presented. The restaurant is a great option for a special occasion because of its lovely garden setting, which enhances the entire eating experience.

4. **Ristorante Alle Darsene di Loppia**: Situated in Tremezzo, this restaurant offers great food in addition to a lovely lakefront setting. This restaurant, which is housed in a historic building that was formerly a boathouse, provides a sophisticated atmosphere for a get-together with friends or a romantic evening. Their cuisine showcases the best foods in the area with a blend of creative and classic meals. Savor delicious seafood, freshly cooked pasta, and decadent desserts while taking in Lake Como's calm beauty.

5. **Bar Il Molo**: Visit Bar Il Molo in Menaggio for a more relaxed

eating atmosphere. This lively café on the lake provides a varied menu of pizzas, sandwiches, and salads along with a relaxed ambiance. It's a well-liked place to unwind and take in the atmosphere of Lake Como, whether you're having a leisurely lunch or a quick nibble. This is because of the welcoming service and stunning views.

6. **Trattoria Baita Belvedere:** Situated amidst the mountains that overlook Bellagio, this eatery provides a distinctive dining encounter accompanied by stunning vistas. This quaint restaurant, which can be reached after a short drive or a beautiful trek, offers regionally influenced traditional meals. Savor substantial meals like polenta, roasted meats, and wild animals while taking in the tranquil surroundings of Lake Como. This trattoria is the ideal choice for a great supper because of its warm interior and friendly personnel.

7. **Gelateria Lariana**: An excursion to Lake Como wouldn't be complete without indulging in the smooth, decadent gelato. Both residents and tourists love Como's Gelateria Lariana. Gelateria Lariana is a haven for gelato enthusiasts, offering an extensive range of flavors ranging from traditional favorites to inventive innovations. Savor a cone or cup of their flavor-bursting, velvety-smooth gelato, which is produced with premium ingredients. Gelateria Lariana can satiate your sweet tooth whether you choose a rich chocolate pleasure or a refreshing fruit sorbet.

8. **Crotto dei Platani:** This quaint eatery is tucked away in Brienno, in the shadow of old plane trees. Specializing in authentic Lombard food, this family-run restaurant has a rustic

and pleasant setting. Every meal, from rich stews and slow-cooked meats to homemade pasta and local cheeses, is produced with love and attention to detail. Both locals and tourists love Crotto dei Platani because of its attentive service and friendly atmosphere.

9. **Pasticceria Poletti:** Pasticceria Poletti in Como is a must-visit for everyone who has a fondness for pastries and baked goods. Since 1920, residents have been delighted by the delicious selection of cakes, pastries, and cookies that this charming pastry store has been serving. Pasticceria Poletti serves a variety of delicacies to entice your taste buds, including their original torta Paradiso and classic Italian pastries like cannoli and sfogliatelle. For the ultimate Italian delight, pair this treat with a freshly prepared espresso.

10. **Agriturismo La Fiorida**: Agriturismo La Fiorida in Dubino is the place to go if you want a real farm-to-table experience. This agriturismo, housed in a renovated farmhouse from the 17th century, provides a special chance to enjoy local cuisine while taking in the breathtaking views of the surrounding countryside. Savor a relaxed dinner created with products from their farm, such as freshly picked veggies, housemade cheeses, and meats that are farmed nearby. Every item on the seasonal menu is certain to be overflowing with flavor and freshness, reflecting the varying harvests.

As you sample Lake Como's gastronomic offerings, don't forget to enjoy the leisurely and informal Italian dining atmosphere. Spend some time enjoying every mouthful, strike up a discussion with the welcoming inhabitants, and let the flavors take you right into the center of this amazing area.

With a wide variety of eateries to suit every preference and price range, Lake Como boasts everything from elegant restaurants to intimate trattorias and little cafés. The food experiences in Lake Como are guaranteed to make a lasting impression and produce treasured memories of your time spent in this culinary paradise, whether you're indulging in traditional regional meals, drinking espresso at a café by the lake, or treating yourself to gelato.

26

Shopping and Souvenirs

Regional goods and Crafts
You'll find the local products and crafts of Lake Como, excellent and irresistible when exploring this enchanting region. Lake Como, which is surrounded by gorgeous scenery and quaint towns, provides plenty of chances to indulge in a distinctive shopping experience. Experience this alluring destination's rich tradition and inventiveness via artisanal crafts and premium goods.

1. **Silk**: Lake Como is well-known for producing silk, with a history that dates back to the fifteenth century. The temperature in the area is ideal for agriculture, and there are plenty of mulberry trees in the area. Many silk companies and shops selling a variety of silk goods can be found in Como. Lake Como's silk products are sought after for their flawless quality and classic elegance, ranging from opulent scarves and ties to sophisticated gowns and home furnishings.

2. **Pottery and Ceramics**: Bellagio, a town in Lake Como, is

especially well-known for its manufacturing of pottery and ceramics, which have a strong history in the region. Generation after generation of artists use these traditional skills to create breathtaking creations that perfectly encapsulate the spirit of the area. Lake Como's pottery and ceramics, which range from exquisitely hand-painted plates and bowls to ornamental tiles and vases, capture the vivid hues and natural splendor of the region, making them ideal mementos to adorn your home.

3. **Leather goods:** Lake Como is home to some of the best leather craftspeople in all of Italy. Explore the cobblestone alleyways of Lecco, Bellagio, or Como to find artisan workshops and shops featuring a wide selection of leather goods. The expert craftspeople of Lake Como make sure that every item, from chic purses and wallets to belts and shoes, is painstakingly made with attention to detail, producing durable and attractive accessories.

4. **Woodworking and Inlaid Furniture**: Lake Como has a rich tradition of woodworking and inlaid furniture. Skilled artisans use age-old methods to make magnificent pieces, fusing various wood species to create complex designs. These works of art, which range from elaborate jewelry boxes and furniture to beautiful wall panels, highlight the area's skillful artisans and painstaking attention to detail. Having a piece of Lake Como woodwork is like owning an artistic creation that perfectly captures the essence of the region.

5. **Olive Oil and Regional Specialties**: Lake Como's microclimate and rich soil make it the perfect place to grow olives, which leads to the production of excellent olive oil. Explore the distinct tastes and fragrances of the olive oils in the area by visiting

nearby farms and olive groves. A variety of other regional specialties, including wines, preserves, honey, and handmade cheeses, are also available. These culinary treats offer a delicious flavor of Lake Como's culinary history, making them perfect gifts or souvenirs for foodies.

Marketplaces and Retail Centers

When it comes to shopping, Lake Como provides a fascinating fusion of contemporary shopping centers and historic marketplaces, resulting in a lively retail environment. This gorgeous area of Italy offers something to suit any shopper's taste, whether they are looking for local artists, designer boutiques, or quaint marketplaces. Here, we'll take you to some of the most well-liked marketplaces and shopping centers near Lake Como, where you can treat yourself to an unforgettable shopping experience.

1. **Como City Center:** The biggest city on Lake Como, Como is a shopping haven for compulsives. Its charming squares and winding lanes make up the historic core, which is home to several boutiques, high-end retailers, and regional artisanal shops. The major shopping route, Via Vittorio Emanuele II, is dotted with upscale clothing retailers, jewelry stores, and chic boutiques. Wander through the quaint alleyways at your leisure to unearth hidden gems offering distinctive apparel, accessories, and home decor.

2. **Bellagio**: Bellagio is renowned for its exquisite boutiques and sophisticated charm. Boutiques selling high-end apparel, accessories, and shoes along the charming waterfront promenade. Fashion fans will find a refuge on the major shopping route,

Via Garibaldi, which boasts both local stores and well-known Italian labels. Specialty shops in Bellagio offer artisanal goods manufactured with great care, including handcrafted jewelry, ceramics, and leather goods.

3. **Cernobbio:** Another well-liked location for shopping is Cernobbio. The main thoroughfare, Via Regina, is lined with chic boutiques, vintage stores, and art galleries. Reputable designers' excellent apparel, accessories, and shoes are available here. Numerous excellent interior design stores and antique merchants can be found in Cernobbio, making it a great place for anyone looking for distinctive home furniture and decor. Stroll down the side streets to find secret stores selling handcrafted goods, fine foods, and mementos.

4. **Lenno Market:** The Lenno Market is particularly noteworthy because of its varied selection and lovely surroundings. This market, which takes place every Tuesday along the lakefront promenade, is a sensory delight. Look around booths stocked with locally produced foods, handicrafts, clothes, shoes, and accessories. The market is a sanctuary for collectors and vintage fans because it also has a section devoted to antique and vintage goods. As you shop for one-of-a-kind items, take in the stunning views of Lake Como and the vibrant environment.

5. **Weekly Markets:** The vivid and genuine shopping experience is provided by Lake Como's weekly markets. Every village along the lake hosts these markets, and they are all charming in their unique way. Tuesdays and Thursdays are market days in Como, where a variety of products are sold, such as apparel, accessories, home goods, and fresh vegetables. Wednesdays are market

days in Bellagio, with vendors offering apparel, accessories, handmade goods, and regional cuisine. Furthermore, a lot of the smaller villages near Lake Como have their weekly markets where you can get a taste of the local way of life and find some really interesting finds.

6. **Silk Factory Outlets:** Those who are interested in this magnificent fabric should visit the silk factory outlets in Lake Como, which is known for its silk production. There are numerous stores in the city of Como where you may purchase premium silk goods at deeply discounted costs. Discover the stores to peruse an extensive assortment of exquisitely crafted silk accessories such as ties, scarves, clothes, and home furnishings. Beautiful things are available for both personal use and as excellent presents for close ones.

V

Day Trips and Excursions

27

Lugano

Lugano, a charming Swiss city perched on the northern beaches of Lake Lugano, is an ideal day trip destination from Lake Como. Lugano, a city well-known for its breathtaking natural beauty, lively cultural scene, and extensive history, skillfully blends Swiss efficiency with Italian charm.

L ugano has an amazing location with Lake Lugano's crystal-clear waters and mountains surrounding it. The

Lungolago, the city's charming promenade, provides breathtaking views of the lake and the far-off Swiss Alps. To appreciate Lugano's natural splendor, take a stroll down the promenade, unwind on one of the many benches, or take a boat trip on the lake.

Numerous cultural assets that highlight Lugano's rich legacy may be found there. The city's historic center is home to quaint squares, winding streets, and exquisitely restored structures. See the magnificent frescoes and artworks within the magnificent Lugano Cathedral, a beautiful church built in the Renaissance style.

The Museum of Art (Museo d'Arte), which features a varied collection of modern and contemporary art, is a must-see for art fans. In addition, European and Swiss artwork from the 19th and 20th centuries is on show at the Cantonal Art Museum (Museo Cantonale d'Arte).

Enjoy peace and quiet in Parco Ciani, the biggest park in Lugano, away from the bustle of the city. This verdant haven offers a tranquil haven for those who enjoy the outdoors and stretches alongside the lake. Admire the rare plant varieties, meander around the well-kept gardens, and unwind by the lake. Throughout the summer, the park holds some activities and concerts, which enhances the lively mood.

Climb Monte San Salvatore or Monte Brè for amazing 360-degree views of Lugano and the surrounding area. Experience breathtaking views as you ascend these mountains via a funicular or stroll. Take the ideal picture-perfect shots, have a picnic in the middle of the forest, or eat at a restaurant perched atop a mountain and take in the breathtaking views.

Shopping in Lugano is a lovely experience because of the pedestrianized Via Nassa. Designer boutiques, luxury jewelry stores, and watch shops from Switzerland line this exquisite strip. Peruse the upscale fashion labels, fine Swiss chocolates and pastries, and treat yourself to some retail therapy.

Lugano's culinary scene is a gastronomic delight for the senses when it comes to dining. Savor the local cuisine's blend of Italian and Swiss flavors. Sample some of the area's delicacies, like polenta, risotto, and Swiss cheese dishes. In one of the charming cafés, don't forget to sample the delicious Swiss chocolates and sip on a freshly produced cup of Swiss coffee.

All year long, Lugano is the site of several festivals and cultural events. The summertime Lugano Festival features jazz and classical events as well as other international musical acts. The well-known Lugano Jazz Festival is another event held in the city that draws well-known performers from all over the world. Enjoy the rich cultural tapestry of Lugano and lose yourself in the lively atmosphere of these events.

28

Milan

For those looking for a mix of modernity, culture, and history, Milan, a cosmopolitan city close to Lake Como, makes for an enthralling day trip option. Milan, the financial and fashion hub of Italy, offers a wide range of activities, including world-class museums, well-known retail areas, and breathtaking architectural landmarks.

Milan is a city rich in history, as seen by its magnificent buildings. The most famous feature in the city is the beautiful Gothic church known as the Duomo di Milano.

Wondering at its exquisite features, visitors can explore its stunning interior and ascend to the rooftop for panoramic views.

The Galleria Vittorio Emanuele II, one of the oldest shopping centers in the world with stunning architecture and exclusive businesses, is right next to the Duomo. Explore its sophisticated hallways, indulge in opulent shopping, or enjoy a cup of espresso at one of its little cafes.

Milan is a city rich in cultural attractions, with many top-notch museums and art galleries. Italian Renaissance masters such as Raphael, Caravaggio, and Bellini have pieces in the Pinacoteca di Brera's magnificent collection. In addition, the museum has a lovely courtyard that offers a tranquil haven in the middle of the city.

La Scala is a must-visit location for opera fans. One of the most famous opera theaters in the world, La Scala presents amazing shows and has an opera museum that provides information about the background and customs of Italian opera.

The Last Supper(Il Cenacolo).), a masterwork by Leonardo da

Vinci, is a must-see attraction for every trip to Milan. This famous mural, which is kept in the refectory of the Convent of Santa Maria delle Grazie, shows the biblical scene of the Last Supper. Access is restricted because of its sensitive nature, therefore it's best to purchase tickets well in advance.

Milan is a sanctuary for those who love fashion because it is known as the capital of the world's fashion. The Fashion Quadrangle, also known as the Quadrilatero della Moda, is a district that features opulent shops, flagship stores, and designer showrooms that present the newest designs and trends from well-known fashion businesses. Within this fashion hotspot, you may revel in a world of style and elegance on the main streets of Via Montenapoleone, Via della Spiga, and Corso Venezia.

Discovering Milan's food scene is a pleasure in and of itself. The city provides a wide variety of gastronomic experiences, from chic cafes and fine dining facilities to classic trattorias providing real Milanese cuisine. Take advantage of the chance to sample regional favorites like cotoletta alla Milanese, breaded veal cutlet, or risotto alla Milanese, a risotto enhanced with saffron. Savor the culinary treats of the city and wash it down with a glass of Lombardia wine.

Visit the Navigli neighborhood, which is well-known for its charming canals and exciting nightlife, for a singular experience. Discover the quaint alleyways beside the canal that are lined with hip bars, boutiques, and art galleries. The well-liked Navigli Antique Market takes place in the neighborhood on the final Sunday of each month. There, you may peruse stands brimming with antiques, furniture, and treasures.

29

Bergamo

S ituated in the Lombardy area of Italy, Bergamo is a gorgeous city that is easily accessible from Lake Como. Bergamo, which is split into the lively Città Bassa (Lower Town) and the enchanted Città Alta (Upper Town), offers a distinctive fusion of contemporary energy and historic elegance.

Start your discovery of Bergamo at the Città Alta, the city's old center and a UNESCO World Heritage Site. This medieval neighborhood, encircled by historic Venetian walls, is a veritable gold mine of stunning buildings, cobblestone streets, and quaint piazzas.

Commence at Piazza Vecchia, the principal plaza featuring exquisite Renaissance architecture. Climb the Torre del Campanone for sweeping views of the city, and visit the historic Palazzo della Ragione, home to the renowned Colleoni Chapel.

Palazzo della Ragione

Admire the magnificent specimen of Lombard Romanesque architecture, the Basilica of Santa Maria Maggiore. Beautiful tapestries and elaborate murals cover the interior.

A visit to the Rocca di Bergamo is essential for history buffs. The Museo del Risorgimento, which is devoted to the history of the Italian unification movement, is housed in this historic stronghold, which commands impressive views of the surrounding countryside.

descend to Bergamo's modern Città Bassa neighborhood. This thriving neighborhood is well-known for its colorful squares, commerce avenues, and cultural landmarks.

The Accademia Carrara is a well-known art gallery with an impressive collection of Italian Renaissance and Baroque masterpieces that art enthusiasts should not miss. Admire pieces by Raphael, Titian, and Botticelli, among others.

Wander down Sentierone, a tree-lined boulevard dotted with eateries, stores, and cafes. Enjoy some shopping therapy and take in the local atmosphere on this bustling pedestrian street.

Bergamo is a culinary paradise, renowned for its delicious traditional delicacies. Savor regional specialties like polenta taragna (buckwheat polenta), casoncelli (stuffed pasta), and the well-known tiramisu made in the Bergamo way. Don't pass up this opportunity to indulge. Enjoy a glass of the excellent Franciacorta wine, which is made in the neighboring Lombardy region, with your dinner.

Go to San Vigilio Hill for sweeping views of Bergamo. Enjoy breath-blowing views of the city, the surrounding countryside, and the far-off Alps by taking a stroll up the hill or riding the funicular. Discover the quaint village perched on the hill, pay a visit to the remnants of the medieval castle, and unwind in the tranquil surroundings of nature.

Bergamo offers a lively and engaging experience all year round with some festivals and cultural events. Celebrated opera composer Gaetano Donizetti is the subject of the Donizetti Opera Festival, which takes place in historic locations throughout the city. The world's jazz fans come to the Bergamo Jazz Festival, which presents world-class musicians in a variety of moody settings.

VI

Itinerary suggestions

30

Romantic Weekend Getaways

H ere's a romantic weekend schedule for a wonderful getaway at Lake Como:

Day 1: Arrival and Romantic Stroll

Morning:
   - Arrive in Como Town and check into a beautiful lakeside hotel or villa.

Afternoon:
   - Take a leisurely walk through the lovely streets of Como. - Visit the Como Cathedral for its architectural grandeur and quiet environment.

Evening: Romantic Dinner by the Lake

- Enjoy a romantic supper at a lakefront restaurant, eating Italian cuisine while admiring the sunset over Lake Como.

Day 2: Elegant Villas and Scenic Views

Morning:
   Take a ferry to Bellagio, regarded as the "Pearl of Lake Como."
Explore the charming lanes and alleys filled with handcrafted businesses.

Afternoon:
   - Wander through the magnificent Villa Melzi Gardens, replete with charming walkways and breathtaking views of the lake.

Evening:
   - Arrange for a private boat excursion on Lake Como, complete with champagne and stunning views as the sun sets over the water.

Day 3: Serene Retreat and Departure

Morning:
   - Enjoy a leisurely morning in a spa, indulging in couples' massages or wellness treatments.

Afternoon:
   Have a leisurely lakeside lunch, relishing local foods and soaking in the tranquil ambiance.

Evening:
   Depart from Lake Como with cherished recollections of a romantic and wonderful weekend break.

This schedule is designed to provide a great blend of romantic activities, from exploring beautiful villages and magnificent villas to soaking in gorgeous vistas and moments of relaxation, assuring a wonderful weekend for you and your spouse at Lake Como.

31

Explore Lake Como in One Week

H ere's a proposed one-week schedule for a first-time
visitor enjoying the delights of Lake Como:

Day 1: Arrival in Como

- Morning: Arrive at Como Town and check into accommodations.
- Afternoon: Explore the historic center of Como. Visit the Como Cathedral and take a stroll along the lovely streets.
- Evening: Enjoy dinner at a small trattoria by the lakefront.

Day 2: Bellagio and Villa Melzi Gardens

- Morning: Take a ferry to Bellagio, the Pearl of Lake Como. Explore the town's small lanes and boutique stores.
- Afternoon: Visit the lovely Villa Melzi Gardens with its stunning lake views and quiet ambiance.
- Evening: Return to Como for dinner and relax by the

lakefront.

Day 3: Varenna and Castello di Vezio

- Morning: Travel to Varenna, a lovely village. Explore its lovely streets and see the lakeside promenade.
- Afternoon: Hike up to Castello di Vezio for panoramic views of Lake Como and see the historic fortification.
- Evening: Enjoy dinner at a local trattoria in Varenna.

Day 4: **Tremezzo and Villa Carlotta**

- Morning: Visit Tremezzo and view the beautiful Villa Carlotta with its botanical gardens.
- Afternoon: Relax in the gardens and have a picnic lunch.
- Evening: Return to Como for dinner and perhaps a leisurely evening stroll.

Day 5: Menaggio and Water Activities

- Morning: Travel to Menaggio and visit its lovely squares and lakeside cafés.
- Afternoon: Enjoy water sports like kayaking or paddleboarding on Lake Como.
- Evening: Experience a lakeside supper in

Day 6: Off-the-Beaten-Path Adventure

- Morning: Venture off the beaten route to uncover hidden hamlets or visit small markets for unique items.
- Afternoon: Relax at a secluded beach or take a lovely nature stroll.
- Evening: Enjoy a nice dinner at a local family-run trattoria.

Day 7: Relaxation and Departure

- Morning: Relax by the lakeside, possibly with a morning coffee and gorgeous views.
- Afternoon: Last-minute exploration or souvenir shopping.
- Evening: Departure from Lake Como.

This itinerary offers a mix of touring iconic towns, enjoying cultural and natural sights, delighting in local food, and embracing the peacefulness of Lake Como—a fantastic introduction to the region's beauty and charm for first-time visitors

Made in the USA
Las Vegas, NV
09 February 2024

85507862R00085